RUMINATIONS
ON THE
DISTORTION OF OIL PRICES
AND CRONY CAPITALISM

RAYMOND J. LEARSY

RUMINATIONS ON THE DISTORTION OF OIL PRICES AND CRONY CAPITALISM

Selected Writings

iUniverse LLC
Bloomington

RUMINATIONS ON THE DISTORTION OF OIL PRICES AND CRONY CAPITALISM
SELECTED WRITINGS

iUniverse books may be ordered through booksellers or by contacting:

iUniverse
1663 Liberty Drive
Bloomington, IN 47403
www.iuniverse.com
1-800-Authors (1-800-288-4677)

ISBN: 978-1-4759-9451-3 (sc)
ISBN: 978-1-4759-9452-0 (hc)
ISBN: 978-1-4759-9453-7 (e)

Library of Congress Control Number: 2013910786

Printed in the United States of America

iUniverse rev. date: 7/3/2013

Author photo:
TIMOTHY GREENFIELD-SANDERS

O liberté! O liberté! Que de crimes on commet en ton nom!

—Mme. Roland, on her way to the guillotine
November 8, 1793

[**AUTHOR'S NOTE:** *Translation with poetic license,* "Free enterprise! Free enterprise! What crimes are committed in thy name!"]

ALSO BY RAYMOND J. LEARSY

Over A Barrel: Breaking Oil's Grip on Our Future

Oil and Finance: The Epic Corruption 2006-2010

Oil and Finance: The Epic Corruption Continues 2010-2012

Contents

ACKNOWLEDGMENTS

First, my thanks to my ever-patient wife, Melva Bucksbaum, who assiduously and cheerfully served as my editor in chief these many months, in spite of my temperament and for which I am forever grateful.

And also my deep thanks to my administrative assistant, Beth Rybczyk, for her unflinching assistance and help in navigating the flood of compositional minutiae that comprise the contents of this book.

INTRODUCTION

Any attempt to weaken oil's stranglehold on our economy, our environment, and our national security will be treated by oil's beneficiaries as an act of aggression, even approaching an act of war. I have tried to make readers clearly understand all this in my various previous commentaries, and again here throughout this book. The great ally of oil interests, both commercial and political, is misinformation. Specifically, misinformation served up in amplitude. This lulls all to sleep by encouraging them to believe blindly in the efficacy of the marketplace: that the price of oil and its availability are standards derived from a free market responding to the true vectors of supply and demand. This is not the case, and herein lies the tale of these ruminations as they apply to the oil industry, its flacks, much of the financial sector wedded to the oil mavens, our bought-and-paid-for government, and its quiescent oversight agencies. In addition to this, of course, are the enabling commodity exchanges and their malign role as the roulette wheel to the distortions of oil and oil product pricing (gasoline, heating oil, and so on) paid for out of the pockets of America's everyman and -woman.

The commentary in this book not only touches on the distortion of oil pricing but also on the grotesque distortions of the crony capitalism that has enriched the few and left Main Street in the lurch, largely as a result of government mismanagement, moneyed influence, and craven oversight. The damage of crony capitalism reaches into the very sinews of our lives. The writings collected in this book show how speculators—and all too often government-backed investment banks with proprietary trading desks and access to near limitless funding through the Federal Reserve or from the federally insured monies of their depositors (monies ironically deposited for safekeeping)—ratchet up the prices of the basic material goods essential to our daily lives, such as gasoline and foodstuff, thereby ceding the determination of those prices not to the laws of supply and demand but predominantly to gambling dens on the trading floors of our balefully unmonitored commodity exchanges.

When he appeared before the Senate Committee on Government Affairs as long ago as November 1, 1990, Leon Hess, a prominent figure in the oil world and the heralded founder and chairman of Hess Oil, testified, "I'm an old man, but I'd bet my life that if the Merc [New York Mercantile Exchange] was not in operation, there would be ample oil and reasonable prices all over the world, without this volatility."[1]

Flash forward twenty-one years, when Rex Tillerson, the CEO and chairman of ExxonMobil, the world's largest publicly owned oil company, testified before the Senate Finance Committee on May 12, 2011. In answer to Senator Maria Cantwell's (D-WA) incisive questioning,[2] Mr. Tillerson stated that the price of oil should be $60/barrel to $70/barrel, or $30 to $40 less than the price of nearly $100/barrel quoted on the commodity exchanges at that time.

During those hearings, commentators pointed out that speculation has vast impact on price distortions, wherein more than 70 percent of oil trading on the commodity exchanges is done not by producers or consumers, rationally hedging their production or consumption needs, but by speculators/traders who neither produce nor consume the oil they trade through the exchanges. Exploring the ramifications of these issues, this book's commentary touches on the reasons why we accept these unconscionable distortions in spite of the enormous cost to the body public. To frame all this in quantifiable terms, some twenty million barrels/day are consumed in the United States, which, at Tillerson's lesser $30/barrel figure, brings a bonanza of an additional $600 million/day, or $219 billion/year, to oil interests. And that is just out of the pockets of American consumers. It is one of the greatest heists of all time, and it represents a massive failure of governance and oversight, while simultaneously exposing the complicity of a somnolent press.

Most pointedly, this book's collected ruminations touch on Wall Street's corrupting influence on the price of oil/gasoline and other commodities. Not to be left out of the picture are the policy distortions, or lack thereof, influenced by the industry itself and foisted upon our political representatives, as well as our ineffectual government agencies, be it the Commodity Futures Trading Commission (CFTC), the Department of Energy (DOE), Congress, and even our courts and their jejune interpretation of sovereign immunity, which gives the OPEC cartel's national oil companies free rein to roll over us.

Along with commentary on OPEC's oil production and pricing machinations, this book's ruminations also touch on the malevolent impact of oil's massive revenue stream in the indoctrination of jihadist dogma and the grim political upheaval and messianic fanaticism touching so much of the world, from the formation of the Taliban to the horrors of Mali—not to mention 9/11.

This compilation of writings is meant to provide an overview of the basic and important theme described above: our enslavement to oil and the money inextricably tied to it. The book's format is meant to enhance the subject matter by providing both the means to further an understanding and to engage in coherent and meaningful discussion. The book's focus may meander occasionally to issues of concurrent interest, with general observations on the following topics: energy independence; national security; politics; shale gas and oil; fracking; commodity exchanges; OPEC; the US Department of Energy (DOE); the Federal Reserve; the Strategic Petroleum Reserve (SPR). To some extent, the writings do repeat issues, but only insofar as many of the themes are so interrelated that they overlap. However, any repetitions are meant to reemphasize importance and to clarify and substantiate the underpinnings of the observations at hand.

Much is written with a touch of what I consider rightful anger. Anger that rises from my years of experience in the commodities trading field. I have written extensively on these issues and witnessed the distortions brought about by the transmutation of trading in physical commodities to trading in commodity future derivatives on the Commodities Exchanges (what I have termed "paper barrels"). Together with the malign impact of lobbying by both the powerful oil industry and Wall Street, all this has distorted government policy, crippling Main Street in the process.

Add to this mix the vast distortion to the free market occasioned by the sinister machinations of the OPEC oil cartel, which was the subject of my earlier book, *Over A Barrel: Breaking the Middle East Oil Cartel*. Clearly, I am not alone in feeling rightful anger, as that book elicited such comments as:

> This book provides a very insightful analysis of the powerful grip that OPEC has over a very important natural resource, why there is no shortage of oil, and why oil prices should be much lower. It also provides all the necessary rationale for standing and defeating this economic evil.
>
> —Henry Kaufman
> President of Henry Kaufman & Company
> Author of *The Road to Financial Reformation: Warnings, Consequences, Reforms*

Finally, I believe that a knowledgeable consumer is a powerful consumer, and these collected writings are meant to contribute to that knowledge.

[**AUTHOR'S NOTE:** *The date of the original blog post appears at the start of each piece. Please refer to these throughout in order to remain aware of the chronology of the writing.*]

THE *NEW YORK TIMES* CONTINUES TO PUMP UP THE PRICE OF OIL, MUCH TO THE OIL INDUSTRY'S JOY

Posted: 01/02/12, 5:04 AM EST

No critical commodity moves as much on rhetoric, rather than supply-and-demand fundamentals, as does crude oil. Over the years few news services, perceived as being disinterested purveyors of news and information, have lent their imprimatur more to the upward distortion of oil prices than the *New York Times*.

In keeping with what now has become a sorry tradition, the *New York Times* on Thursday gave the oil patch and its allied interests good reason to pop champagne corks two days early in celebration of the New Year. Assuming a mantle of authority, the *New York Times* presented to its readership, packaged in the babble of well-honed oil industry mantras and conveyed to us as received wisdom from on high, illuminations the likes of which a well-oiled oil industry flack would have been embarrassed to disseminate. The good scribes of the *Times*, in their lead story in the business section, told us with the headline, "Oil Prices Predicted to Stay above $100 a Barrel through Next Year".[3]

The article ends with this: "Consumers have this belief that prices will either go up or they will remain at elevated levels." The reportage fills three-quarters of a *New York Times* page, regaling us with reasons why, at the very least, "elevated levels" will remain; all with the subtext that we should celebrate such an outcome, as prices might very well go higher. This kind of reporting undoubtedly had the oil gang cheering, as they recently reported bottom line record earnings with those oil prices at "current" levels. Meanwhile, the rest of the country is still in a deep funk.

The article also made us feel better by pointing out that "The United States economy managed to cope this year despite triple digit prices for barrels of oil." Such is the information we are fed by the *New York Times* scribes, seemingly safe at their business desk sinecures, frighteningly oblivious to a near 9 percent countrywide unemployment rate and the millions out of work, not to mention the millions evicted from their foreclosed homes, none of whom seem to "cope" with the prevailing circumstances in the least.

Other than its references to the playing out of foreign policy issues, such as Iran's threat to blockade the Strait of Hormuz and all that would entail, the *Times* hastens to instruct us that oil prices have an innate right to hover at their current astronomical heights. This perspective becomes clear when the *Times* states that "Many governments in the Middle East spent heavily on social assistance programs in response to the unrest of the Arab Spring and are depending on higher prices to meet their budgets." Now, does that make you feel warmer up there in Maine?

And when it comes to higher prices, there is no mention of the breakdown of our oversight agencies, such as the Commodity Futures Trading Commission (CFTC) and its failure to rein in excessive speculation in oil prices. [Please see "Time to Dismiss the CFTC Chairman and His Commissioners," *Huffington Post* (blog), December 27, 2010.[4]] This is not just my layman's opinion.

Much more significantly, it is also the opinion of Rex Tillerson, CEO of the world's largest oil giant, ExxonMobil. To his great credit, during his testimony before the Senate Finance Committee in May 2011, Tillerson expressed his exasperation that the then current price of oil at $100/barrel incorporated some $30 to $40 of its price as a result of speculation. [Please see "Are Our Leaders Hearing ExxonMobil CEO Rex Tillerson?" *Huffington Post* (blog), May 17, 2011.[5]]

Nor did the article make any reference to that fundamental game changer: the vast deposits of low-cost natural gas. Through new drilling techniques, such as environmentally evolving fracking, enormous reservoirs of shale gas have been identified in dimensions barely understood just a few years ago; enough to meet domestic needs for the next 150 years. The potential is so large, a consensus is building that it will lead to American energy independence.

In years past, oil and natural gas prices moved up and down in near lockstep. Such was the case when oil prices peaked at $147/barrel in the summer of 2008 (helping to bring on the housing crisis and the financial meltdown in September of that year). The price of natural gas at that time was near $15.00/MMbtu (one million British thermal units, the term used to measure heat and energy). Today, while the price of oil rests near $100/barrel, as quoted on the New York Mercantile Exchange (NYMEX) for West Texas Intermediate (WTI), the price of natural gas has dropped to under $3.00/MMBtu. At that price for natural gas, the comparable energy quotient in a barrel of oil would bring its price down to less than $20/barrel. Clearly, with a differential of this magnitude and with natural gas being environmentally friendlier than oil-based commodities like gasoline, some substitution will begin to weigh on the consumption of oil, whether in home heating or converting trucks to natural gas fuel rather than gasoline/diesel. It is a trend only beginning now that will have major impact on the need for and consumption of crude oil in the years ahead.

Yet, here again, instead of reporting clearly on this development and its enormous potential, the *New York Times* engaged in reportage bordering on yellow journalism [please see "New York Times Flays Natural Gas ..." June 28, 2011[6]], including two articles filled with conjecture bordering on disinformation: "Insiders Sound an Alarm Amid a Natural Gas Rush"[7] (June 25, 2011) and "Behind Veneer, Doubt on Future of Natural Gas"[8] (June 26, 2011). Furthermore, this reportage places the entire shale gas revolution into question, interjecting such terminology as "Ponzi scheme," "dot-com bubble," and so on. This in the face of billions of dollars invested in the shale gas and shale oil plays by such "doubters" as ExxonMobil, Shell, Chevron, Statoil (the Norwegian national oil company), CNOOC (the oil company owned by the Chinese government), and Total (the French oil behemoth). The list goes on. But the *Times* instructed us otherwise, thereby helping to keep oil prices on the ascent by vesting us with the ignorance needed to accept high and manipulated oil prices unquestioningly.

It has been a tradition of distortion or misinformation dating back years—whether sweeping the manipulations of OPEC under the rug, or heralding the pronouncements of that oil price manipulator par excellence and OPEC's premier protagonist Saudi Arabia, without a questioning eye. [Please see "The New York Times Continues Its Fawning Coverage of Saudi Oil Policies," March 22, 2010.[9]]

Sadly, the *New York Times*, on the issue of how oil prices are determined, has become a leading apologist of industry excess and government connivance. Its scribes are seemingly oblivious to the distortion of pricing instigated by OPEC, the commodity exchanges and their nurturing of excess speculation, and Wall Street and its feckless proprietary trading financed in large measure through beneficent government programs.

Given its standing and the thrust of its coverage, the *Times* has become an important contributor to the public's baleful acceptance of having its pockets picked by the oil interests the world over.

SEC Alters Enforcement Policy, Too Late for Goldman Sachs and the Nation

Posted: 01/09/12, 3:20 PM EST

One of the most grievous mishandlings by our government's oversight agencies was the botched July 2010 consent judgment of the *SEC v. Goldman Sachs & Co.*, an action brought by the Securities and Exchange Commission (SEC) as part of its statutory oversight responsibilities. The judgment permitting Goldman Sachs to enter a consent decree without admitting or denying the allegations of the complaint was an unbridled sop viewed by too many as a ploy of the good-old-boys network looking after each other[10]. The Abacus instruments Goldman created and then bet against cost its clients hundreds of millions more than the $550 million fine assessed against Goldman in its consent judgment with the SEC; all this while simultaneously setting aside a bonus pool of $23 billion, seemingly derived in part from profits of actions incorporated under the consent decree.

Why touch on this issue now? Because at long last the SEC, which for too long has served as a vassal of powerful Wall Street interests, was denied approval of the proposed consent judgment between the

SEC and Citigroup in late November under the stern and scolding ruling delivered by the ever-wise Judge J. E. Rakoff. The insightful ruling has shamed the SEC into declaring that it would henceforth no longer permit companies that admit criminal wrongdoing to deny the allegations in a parallel civil settlement under a new set of SEC enforcement rules. This occurred in a case that had all the earmarks of the *SEC v. Goldman* settlement just over a year and a half ago.

To quote from Judge Rakoff's opinion and order[11] (SDNY, Opinion and Order, 11-CIV-7387):

> And, most obviously, the proposed consent judgment does not serve the public interest, because it asks the court to employ its power and assert its authority when it does not know the facts.

> An application of judicial powers that does not rest on facts is worse than mindless; it is inherently dangerous. The injunctive power of the judiciary is not a free-roving remedy to be exercised at the whim of a regulatory agency, even with the consent of the regulated. Finally, in any case like this that touched the transparency of financial markets whose gyrations have so depressed our economy and debilitated our lives, there is an overriding public interest in knowing the truth. In much of the world, propaganda reigns, and truth is confined to secretive, fearful whispers. Even in our nation, apologists for suppressing or obscuring the truth may always be found. But the SEC, of all agencies, has a duty, inherent in its statutory mission, to see that the truth emerges; and if it fails to do so, this court must not, in the name of deference or convenience, grant judicial enforcement to the agency's contrivances.

Had these words been entered a year and a half ago when Goldman Sachs reached a settlement with the SEC, much of the anger, much of the frustration of ordinary Americans at the perceived connivance of government and Wall Street, would have been dissipated. Bringing Goldman to the judgment of its citizen peers in a court of law would have been calmingly therapeutic for the nation as a whole, no matter the outcome. But what transpired seemed like a rigged extravaganza, only throwing more fuel on the cauldron of the nation's discontent.

King Abdullah, Why Isn't the OPEC Cabal Responding?

Posted: 01/26/2012, 6:38 AM EST

The Organization of Petroleum Exporting Countries (better known as OPEC) has swept aside your target of what a fair price for oil should be. And perhaps, the worst miscreant in that coven of reprobates is your own benighted subject, Saudi oil minister Ali al-Naimi. The man shows no respect.

Why, not that long ago he brayed to all who would listen that you in your wisdom viewed $75/barrel as a fair price, a price he vested with the term of "noble". [Please see "OPEC's Noble Cause," *Huffington Post* (blog), December 17, 2008.[12]] And just last week he let it be known, clearly in contravention to his monarch's proclamation, that the current price of $100/barrel for oil quoted on the New York Mercantile Exchange (NYMEX) is just fine, and $110/barrel for Brent crude oil quoted in London is even better. [Please see "Saudi Arabia Targets $100 Crude Price," *Financial Times*, January 16, 2012.[13]] This is especially so, we are supposed to understand, because of the big public spending increases needed to forestall the political unrest sweeping the Middle East. Cunningly, he put it in such a way that we should be happy to have oil at these price levels (leading to near $4.00/gallon for gasoline at the pump stateside), considering all the troubles with Iran and the narrow Strait of Hormuz.

King Abdullah, it is not befitting your regal eminence that you are overcut so heedlessly, relegating your royal pronouncements to the dustbin, and it makes us wonder who truly is in charge: you, Your Highness, or your peripatetic oil minister?

Also, Your Highness, this is not good timing. Everyone is concerned about those messianic fanatics situated across from you on the far shore of the Persian Gulf. No telling what they are up to these days. One thing is for sure: were it not for our good ol' US Navy flotilla steaming off your shores in the Persian Gulf, they'd be knocking at your palace door, much to your displeasure; unless of course, you would enjoy being paraded down Main Street in Tehran. And if you tolerate the machinations of your oil minister who pushes the price of oil to levels beyond what you yourself said is a fair price, and he forever waits to bestir it ever higher, the price of your inaction may become intolerably high for you and your many princely cousins.

You see, we have an election coming up here in the United States, with all that may entail. That said, and with this nation's growing volition to disengage our foreign entanglements, we will start to reexamine many of our policies and may decide that the current price of oil—and the much more than $100 million/day it costs the American public to keep a task force in the Persian Gulf to safeguard your coastline—is more than we are willing to handle, and then we may decide that it is time for our task force to weigh anchor and leave you to your own devices.

And in case Mr. Ali al-Naimi didn't tell you, we are on the verge of becoming energy independent. In the last few years, with the development of new drilling techniques, efficient hybrid cars, wind and solar energy, and vast resources of coal, we are quickly veering toward energy independence. To the point, as the development of shale gas and shale oil grows, the United States will become an important exporter of fossil fuels and energy commodities. In natural gas alone, the expansion of proven resources using the new technology is enough to service this nation's needs for 150 years, and that expansion continues to grow.

Your Highness, just in case you have not been doing your sums, consider the following: Natural gas and crude oil were traditionally priced in tandem almost step by step, but with the vast new supplies of natural gas here in the United States, that relationship has now changed dramatically. Natural gas has become so abundant that its price has retreated to levels last seen some ten years ago. Today the price is $2.75/MMBtu, a price at which it delivers an energy quotient equivalent to crude oil priced at less than $17/barrel—that is, levels reflecting quoted crude oil prices of a little over ten years ago!

While your Mr. Ali al-Naimi wants us to pay $100/barrel (and more), please understand that we are not so stupid as to sit idly by. If he wants to keep oil prices at that level, we will have trucks and then cars powered by compressed natural gas (CNG) traveling our roads in short order. [Please see "What Is CNG?" http://www.cngnow.com.[14]]

And please, Your Highness, do not have your Mr. Ali al-Naimi then ask around what he should do with all your oil, as the answer would not be adequately elegant.

Iran's Oil Threat, "Déjà Vu All Over Again"

Posted: 01/30/2012, 5:21 AM EST

Where is Yogi Berra when we need him? There is Iran going back to its old game plan, threatening to ban oil exports. This time, however, Europe is preparing its own import embargo on deliveries of Iranian oil, given the lack of progress in neutralizing Iran's nuclear program.

In retaliation, Iran's Parliament is now working on a plan[15] to stop Iran's ongoing oil exports to Europe forthwith in retaliation for Europe's embargo scheduled to become effective July 1, 2012.

"Europe will burn in the fire of Iran's oil wells" were the threatening words spoken by Nasser Soudani,[16] a member of the Iranian Parliament's energy committee. Mr. Soudani continued, "All European countries that made Iran the target of their sanctions will not be able to buy one drop of oil from Iran."

The rant has the same tonality as that of Iran's Ayatollah Ali Khamenei, who treated the world to a similar proclamation in June 2006[17], then directed mostly at the United States, threatening to curtail energy flows from the region. At the time, Khamenei delivered his threats from a podium emblazoned with the words of his predecessor, Ayatollah Ruhollah Khomeini: "America Cannot Do a Damn Thing."

To repeat observations made then that still hold true today: the International Energy Agency continues to hold some 4.1 billion barrels of strategic and commercial reserves, including the 700-plus million barrels in the US Strategic Petroleum Reserve (SPR), and more than 300 million barrels in commercial reserves in the United States as well.

Iran's current exports of oil to Europe are some 425,000 barrels/day, which comes to 155 million barrels/year, a figure easily made available from standby strategic and commercial reserves.

In addition, there are the assurances by the Gulf oil producers that they will make up the Iranian shortfall. Saudi Arabia, while producing 9.8 million barrels/day currently, has a spare production capacity of 2 million barrels/day on standby, according to CNN, which quoted Saudi oil minister Ali al-Naimi on January 17, 2012: "I believe we can easily get up to 11.8 [million barrels a day] almost immediately, in a few days, because all we need is to turn valves." We can assume that up to another million barrels can be brought onstream in short order. [18]

Iran's total daily export loadings are some 2 million-plus barrels/day. With strategic and commercial reserves in place, and with the significant additional production capability available from the Gulf Arab States (Saudi Arabia, Kuwait, United Arab Emirates [UAE], etc.), we can say: Sorry, Yogi, this time it *is* over *before* it's over!

Maine Freezes While Washington Snoozes

Posted: 02/05/2012, 9:40 AM EST

"Are these people going to be found frozen?" These are words that define what the cold of winter means to so many in Maine. Stark, frightening words from the owner of a small oil dealership listening to the pleas of too many of his customers, unable to pay for their heating oil deliveries—and depicted in a stirring *New York Times* article, "In Fuel Oil Country, Cold That Cuts to the Heart," on January 4, 2012. [19]

The price of heating oil has gone up to $3.71/gallon this year, an increase of $0.40. Meanwhile, Congress and the Obama administration cut the energy assistance program meant to help the poor pay their heating bills. In Maine alone, that covers 65,000 households who must now make do with $483 in assistance, down from $804 a year ago. All this while the major oil companies are raking in humongous record profits!

And all this while Washington snoozes away, letting the oil boys, both here and abroad, walk all over us despite our fellow citizens freezing up in Maine and the many other northern states.

Yes, occasionally lip service is given to the issue of runaway oil prices and the suspicious peculiarities of their formation, where pricing always connects to the oil "oiligopoly's" mantra, "It's all about supply and demand."

To that end, the administration announced the formation of a financial fraud task force, the Oil and Gas Price Fraud Working Group.[20] This panel was established to focus on fraud in the energy markets and to monitor the oil and gas markets for potential criminal violations, i.e., price fixing, manipulation, etc. To date, nearly one year after this brave announcement, nada! Not a peep from Washington, the administration, or the Department of Justice (DOJ), the very agency vested with the responsibility of organizing the task force—nothing.

Nothing from an administration that has sat idly by while, during the three years since its investiture, the price of crude oil, the determiner of the price of all downstream products, from gasoline to heating oil, has increased by more than 200 percent, from the low $30/barrel in February 2009 to $100/barrel today. (You do the numbers: there is more than a $60/barrel difference in price between then and now, multiplied by the nineteen million barrels of daily US consumption). The cost to the nation is immeasurable, in both economic activity and employment, not just in simple dollars and cents.

This administration has a profound lack of understanding of how oil markets function. Nor is there anyone on board who can help navigate the ship of state on this issue. The Department of Energy (DOE), when not handing out hundreds of millions to the likes of the Solyndra project, is totally at sea in dealing with the unforgiving world of the energy markets. Nobel Prize winner Steven Chu, a brilliant physicist, heads the DOE, but he is nonetheless totally out of his element as secretary of energy. Secretary Chu attempts to deal with the rough-and-tumble oil world, but his lack of ability to do so results in his uttering such misguided nonsense from his DOE-secretary perch as, "OPEC is going to do what they're going to do based on their own interests. I quite frankly don't focus on what OPEC should do; I focus on what we should do."[21]

This statement comes from the world's largest consumer of oil, giving the OPEC cartel carte blanche to continue its manipulations to its heart's content, and at our expense.

Combine the ineffectiveness of the DOE with the vapid oversight of oil futures and petroleum products trading on the commodity exchanges, and you have a recipe for disaster. Don't believe me? Then go ask the good and freezing people up there in Maine.[22]

The Volcker Rule and Wall Street's Pliant Media Plant

Posted: 02/15/2012, 7:05 AM EST

There they go again. Wall Street is fighting tooth and nail to emasculate Dodd-Frank (formally known as the Dodd-Frank Wall Street Reform and Consumer Protection Act), focusing its artillery on the Volcker rule: namely, those sections calling for the elimination of proprietary trading by banking institutions. In case you have forgotten, it was the unbridled proprietary trading bundled with sham housing instruments and derivatives and outright speculation that brought us to the near collapse of the financial system in 2008.

According to yesterday's *New York Times*, Wall Street made its broadest assault yet against new regulation on Monday, taking aim at a rule that has come to define the battle over how to police banks in the aftermath of the financial crisis.[23] And there joining the fray was that forever-pliant Wall Street apologist, *New York Times* columnist, and CNBC talking head, Andrew Ross Sorkin, weighing in with a less-than-feeble endorsement of the Volcker rule ("in the long term it makes a lot of sense") while impugning it in the length and breadth of his column.[24]

To underscore the downside of adopting the Volcker rule, he cites that paragon of banking virtue and responsible husbanding of a banking charter, Jamie Dimon, chairman of JPMorgan Chase. Dimon, the very epitome of the type of banker the Volcker rule is meant to protect us, the public, from. With Dimon at its helm, proprietary trading, and all it embodies with its casino mentality, has become perhaps the key aspirational profit center and motivator of his institution. [Please see "Is JPMorgan a Bank or a Government-Funded Casino?," *Huffington Post* (blog), June 9, 2009.]

Sorkin goes on to enlist comments of critics of the Volcker rule, highlighting their collective arguments that removing big banks from making their own bets will remove liquidity from the system, thereby driving up costs. He then brushes aside Volcker's defense[25]: "The restrictions on proprietary trading by commercial banks legislated by the Dodd-Frank Act are not likely to have an effect on liquidity inconsistent with the public interest." Volcker's comments continue, indicating that there should not be a presumption that "ever more liquidity brings a public benefit."

Sorkin then continues to dismissively counter Volcker's position: "Yet Mr. Volcker doesn't offer any explanation for why it won't, except to argue that less liquidity might tamp down speculative trading."

One would think that Mr. Sorkin, with his extensive curriculum vitae (CV) and daily exposure to the workings of the market, needn't have had to dig very deeply to cite the extensive proprietary trading that bank holding companies the likes of JPMorgan, Morgan Stanley, and Goldman Sachs have undertaken, speculating in a vast range of commodities, such as crude oil, copper, etc., as well as other financial instruments.

In crude oil alone, their proprietary trading has helped bring about ever-higher gasoline and heating oil prices, at the public's expense and to the banks' benefit. The banks achieved this feat by chartering massive VLCCs (very large crude carriers), oil tankers of two hundred thousand DWT (dead-weight tons) or more, filling them with millions of barrels of oil at a cost of hundreds of millions, if not billions, of dollars. They then keep the tankers at sea for months at a time to speculate on the prospect of even higher oil prices. In doing so—that is, by taking oil off the market in the front months—they cause the spot price of oil to rise, which means that we all pay more for petroleum-based products, such as gasoline, diesel fuel, heating oil, etc.

As banks, they have access to the Federal Reserve cash window and its diminutive interest rates. Money lent to banks as banks, carries the implicit responsibility of using those funds to assist the economy by lending to businesses and householders, perhaps even renegotiating mortgages, and generally being agents of economic growth. Certainly it does not imply taking money out of the system in order to speculate on oil and other commodities, while simultaneously having those speculative initiatives result in ever-higher prices paid for by the consuming public. And why should the banks not do this? After all, if their speculative positions blow up, there is the government and the old boys' club at the Treasury and the Fed to bail them out.

But, then again, this is not the first time, so we should not be surprised by Mr. Sorkin's reaction. In fact, Mr. Sorkin has come to the defense of Wall Street interests in the guise of knowledgeable commentator many times before. There was also the paean to Goldman Sachs. [Please see "One Crowd Still Loyal to Goldman Sachs," *New York Times*, June 18, 2010.[26]]

To put the icing on the cake, in his column yesterday, Sorkin quotes Jamie Dimon: "Paul Volcker, by his own admission has said he doesn't understand capital markets. He has proven that to me." Spoken like a veritable croupier angered by a paying houseguest who doesn't want to play at his gaming table.

Oil Embargoes, Sherlock Holmes, and the Russian Butler

Posted: 02/20/2012, 8:22 AM EST

I have no smoking gun, but the butler looks very suspicious. Sherlock Holmes is weighing the suspects, questioning why the high price for Brent crude oil, the benchmark for Europe and much of the world, is being quoted on London's exchanges at prices far exceeding the price of West Texas Intermediate (WTI), the US benchmark. WTI is already quoted at the suspiciously high price of \$103/barrel, while Brent crude is pegged even higher, at \$120/barrel—a difference of some \$17/barrel. The oil interests will tell you the same thing—whether they are the oil companies, their financial industry pundits, or the talking heads on television or in the press—simply put, Iran is the wild card, with all its implications for the supply of oil and its price, given its proximity to the Strait of Hormuz.

Set forth in this space some two weeks ago, in the post, "Iran's Oil Threat, Déjà Vu All Over Again," there is ample supply of oil with or without Iran. As Iran's intransigence on matters nuclear continues, its oil exports will be embargoed in a manner similar to Europe's embargo of Syrian oil, and will be replaced by strategic inventories, supplies from Saudi Arabia, the Gulf States, and, yes, you guessed it, Russia.

Russia, currently the world's largest oil producer, is shipping massive quantities of oil, mostly to Europe, but also to the Far East though its extensive, far-flung and expanding network of pipelines. As the *New York Times* reported, "The Russian oil industry was already reaping the rewards of higher oil prices from Iranian tensions."[27] The Russians have been cashing in brilliantly while rendering support to Iran by such acts as vetoing or emasculating any and all meaningful UN resolutions that would force Iran to comply with the terms of the UN's International Atomic Energy Agency mandates. It is an open question whether this is being done in solidarity with Iran, or more malignly, to solidify Iranian intransigence on matters nuclear, in the hope that the European and other world consumers' boycott of Iranian oil has maximum impact, making Russian oil more salable at ever higher prices.

Meanwhile, the tumult and fabricated anxieties over Iran's oil supply provide ample cover for an oil price that veers ever higher—a price explained away by the political tensions at hand. But the question needs to be asked: what is really driving oil prices?

Consider the following. The price of natural gas in the United States is less than $3.00/MMBtu. Russia is a major supplier of natural gas to Western Europe. Russian gas giant Gazprom's contracts with European consumers have an especially onerous clause under current circumstances and conditions. The price of natural gas is calculated in relation to the quoted price of Brent crude, so that at $120 barrel/oil, Europeans are paying some $15.00/MMBtu, significantly more when compared to US consumers, be they homeowners or industrial buyers (e.g., manufacturers of ammonia or nitrogen fertilizers, for which natural gas is the core building block, and that is just one example of industrial use). This is a staggering difference in cost, putting swaths of European industry at enormous disadvantage to their American counterparts.

Clearly, given Russia's growing capability to produce and deliver oil wherever the market dictates, and given the tie between the price of oil and the price of gas in Russian supply contracts, it is in the clear interest of the Russians to push up the price of Brent crude. Therefore, could it be that the tumult around deliveries of Iranian oil is merely a smoke screen to escalate prices, and that something far more nefarious is taking place?

In 2008, this space posted "The Trade That Brought Us $100/Barrel Oil Teaches Us to Be Afraid, Very Afraid," setting forth the circumstances of the trade that caused the price of oil to touch $100/barrel.[28] This trade was implemented by a single trader buying one futures contract covering one thousand barrels of oil, for which he needed a margin deposit of only $6,750. That one trade moved the market by more than $0.40/barrel, a sum that over a day's time would have increased the transfer of wealth to oil interests by some $35 million, calculated on the world's consumption of nearly eight-five million barrels/day at that time. To his great regret, the trader made the vainglorious mistake of boasting about his vanity trade, only to have the CFTC fine his employer, a former division of ConAgra Foods, a massive $12 million, purportedly as a clear message to traders that making a non–bona fide trade to simply move prices was contrary to the commodity exchanges rules. [Please see "US Speculators Fined For $100-a-Barrel 'Vanity Trade,'" The *London Telegraph*, August 18, 2010.][29]

Clearly, it raises the very ominous question, if a single trader, with only $6,750, can move the market, how can you expect those with billions at their disposal not to do the same?

So here we have Russia, a major supplier of oil and gas, with an economy deeply dependent on the revenues received from the sale of those commodities. According to the same New York Times article, "And the taxes the Russian government has received from those sales have been a political windfall for Prime Minister Vladimir V. Putin as he campaigns to return as Russia's president. The extra money has helped further subsidize domestic energy consumption, tamping down inflation." [30] Combine this with a Russia that is in large measure governed by that unique version of our Wall Street good ol' boys network, the alumni of Russia's highly touted secret service, the KGB. The KGB helped form Putin and many of his associates in government. Here was an organization that was the nonpareil master of clandestine intrigue; it knows how to keep secrets, and now in a sense, it is running the country, albeit with the trappings of democratic governance.

Fast-forward to this week: "A group of brokers and traders successfully managed to manipulate an interest rate that affects loans around the world." [Please see "Traders Manipulated Key Rate, Bank Says," *Wall Street Journal,* February 17, 2012. [31]] If this could happen to interest rates, so widely traded throughout the world, just think what a KGB-oriented Russia could do, and not with $6,750 at its disposal, but billions upon billions, and conceivably with the intermediary of the powerful Swiss-based and -protected commodities trading houses, such as the likes of Glencore and Vitol.[32] (Vitol is the largest oil trader in the world.)[33] It should not be a stunning surprise to anyone watching oil prices—be they government agencies, the press, or energy-focused think tanks—that the traded price of Brent crude is being gamed.

Sorry, folks, I don't mean to ruin the ending for you, but that Russian butler does look awfully guilty to Sherlock Holmes!

Mr. President, Now That We Need It, Give Us Our Oil Back

Posted: 02/22/2012, 8:23 AM EST

- Iran is cheering.

- Speculators are profiting.

- Oil producers celebrating.

- Our nascent economic recovery is tottering.

- Household budgets are being ripped apart.

- Homeowners in Maine are freezing.

You are sitting on some seven hundred million barrels of oil in our Strategic Petroleum Reserve (SPR), bought and paid by both the 99 percent and even the 1 percent.

Here we are, living an economic and political emergency, while the tool we have to deal with this issue remains untapped.

A reasonable release from the SPR would immediately drop the price of oil significantly, and, in turn, keep gasoline prices from

23

rising further in the months ahead—and very possibly keep the economic recovery on track. In June 2011, when the Department of Energy (DOE) announced it would release thirty million barrels of oil, the price of oil dropped almost immediately by $4.00/barrel, sending the speculators running for the hills. [Please see "Obama Administration Taps Strategic Petroleum Reserve," *Politico,* June 23, 2011.[34]]

Back then, when the release was announced, Speaker of the House John Boehner bridled[35]:

> Everyone wants to help the American people and lower prices at the pump—especially now, in tough economic times. And it is good that the Obama administration is conceding that increased supply will lower those costs. But by tapping the Strategic Petroleum Reserve, the president is using a national security instrument to address his domestic political problems. The SPR was created to mitigate sudden supply disruptions. This action threatens our ability to respond to a genuine national security crisis and means we must ultimately find the resources to replenish the reserve—at significant cost to taxpayers.

This time around, Mr. Boehner and everyone else should understand that high, and ever higher, oil prices are Iran's most effective weapon. It will help the mullahs realize the cash flow they need to maintain their authoritarian rule while playing nuclear roulette. Embargoing swaths of their oil exports will have little or no impact if their saber rattling, together with the help of the oil speculators, pushes oil prices to ever-higher highs.

Mr. President, pull the plug on the SPR now, and let the oil flow.

The Chicago Mafia, and the Price You Are Paying for Gasoline

Posted: 03/05/2012, 7:57 AM EST

No, no! This is not about the mob holding up service stations and running off with their gas tanks. No, it has the makings of something much more sinister than that, something that has the makings of reaching into all our pockets, making the oil boys rich beyond their wildest dreams while putting the American economy at risk and family budgets in the trash can.

Overlooked, by and large, is the fact that Chicago is to commodity trading what Wall Street is to financial markets. The world's most significant commodity trading exchange, the Chicago Mercantile Exchange Group (CME Group), is headquartered there, does its business there, establishes its policies there, and projects its power to influence institutions, the press, and government from there as the world's leading and most diverse derivatives marketplace. It proudly brays that it is to the CME Group, and, in turn, to Chicago, that "the world comes to manage risk."[36] It is an intrinsic part of Chicago's economy and culture. One could almost say, "as the CME Group goes, so goes Chicago." The *Wall Street Journal* reported: "Chicago-based CME accounts for more than 90 percent of listed US futures trading and has outspent rivals on lobbying in

Raymond J. Learsy

Washington to ensure its views are heard." [Please see "CFTC Suit Marks New Era," *Wall Street Journal*, February 24, 2013.[37]]

That is well and good, but all the while we have in Washington a president whose very political formation was in the sinews of Chicago politics, from his first elected office to his ascent to the White House. And the ties to Chicago continue to be strong, if not even stronger than before.

President Obama's first chief of staff, Rahm Emmanuel, left the White House to run for and be elected mayor of Chicago, where he currently serves. Until the end of last year, the mayor was William M. Daley, secretary of commerce under President Clinton, and former Midwest chairman of JPMorgan Chase, with its overarching business ties, and most significantly, son of the fabled, all-powerful mayor of Chicago, R. J. Daly (mayoral term: 1955–76), and brother of the dauphin mayor of Chicago, Richard M. Daly (mayoral term: 1989–2011). In other words, a man with noble Chicago blood running through his veins.

With these luminaries in place, the CME Group has a head start by a mile in protecting its turf from government interference or otherwise said regulation. It has fought tooth and nail to keep things as they are with massive lobbying and all. This in spite of the growing appreciation throughout the land that commodity exchange trading has distorted, and continues to distort, the norms of supply and demand, extracting an enormous tax on consumers to the benefit of the commodity players, the banks, and their proprietary trading. In the case of the oil industry, commodity trading also results in the transfer of vast riches to the oligopoly of oil producers, funded from the pockets of the many.

And yet, over the years, and certainly during this administration, nothing has been done to rein in the excesses that the commodity exchanges have propagated. The Commodity Futures Trading

Commission (CFTC), with one of its five commissioners being an ex-CME operative, has become the twenty-first-century version of the eighteenth-century castrati, whose talent was to sing beautifully but not do much else, while the CFTC's is to hold hearings endlessly but not do much else. [Please see "Time to Dismiss the CFTC Chairman and His Commissioners," *Huffington Post* (blog), December 27, 2010.[38]] All this is in spite of such power players in the field as Rex Tillerson, chairman and CEO of ExxonMobil (the world's largest publicly traded oil company), telling the Senate Finance Committee in May 2011 that at least 30 to 40 percent of the price of a barrel of oil is the result of speculation. You would have thought the CFTC and the government would have jumped all over that. Yet, a crucial comment of that magnitude was swept under the rug and never to be heard again, probably much to the relief of the CME Group.

There was a bright moment back in April 2011, giving hope that the influence of the Chicago Mafia was giving way to the nation's interest as a whole. Amidst much fanfare was the announcement of the Oil and Gas Price Fraud Working Group, and the prospect of all the skeletons that were about to be uncovered. [Please see "Obama Administration Announces Formation of Oil/Gas Pricing Fraud Panel. Really?" *Huffington Post* (blog), April 27, 2011.[39]] But today, it seems one could readily conjecture that the CME had gotten its tentacles into the heart of that commission, because nothing has been heard from that august body. Next month will be a year since the fanfare of its announcement.

To understand the dimensions and the scope of the CME's trading, one need only refer to its press release of February 8, 2012, barely four weeks ago:

NEW YORK, Feb. 8, 2012 / PR Newswire/ — CME Group, the world's leading and most diverse derivatives marketplace, today announced it set a new record for trading volumes for its energy products on Tuesday, February 7. Trading volume for energy futures and options contracts totaled 3,489,302 contracts yesterday, climbing 13 percent higher than the previous record of 3,098,129 contracts on February 22, 2010. These contracts are listed by and subject to the rules of NYMEX.[40]

Referring to current gasoline prices, President Obama commented in his weekly address but two days ago, "What's happening in Detroit will make a difference (doubling automobile mileage standards by 2025). But it won't solve everything. There is no silver bullet for avoiding spikes in gas prices every year."[41]

No, Mr. President, there is a silver bullet. Go after the commodity exchanges and the distortions to price that they enable. By mandating transparency and both rigid and effective supervision, you could bring down the price of gasoline by one-third in short order. And going one major step further is still achievable within several years' time: by initiating a massive program to convert our transportation vehicles to environmentally safer compressed natural gas (CNG), going on to encourage Detroit to retool, to build a new fleet of cars that run on CNG rather than petroleum-based gasoline.

The price of natural gas closed at $2.48/MMBtu on Friday, March 2. At that price, oil would be forced down to about $15/barrel—yes, $15/barrel!—in order to compete to deliver an equivalent quotient of energy. (Oil closed at $106.74/barrel on Friday, March 2.) Given the new technology that has led to massive and ever-expanding discoveries of natural gas within our borders, what are we waiting for?!

FINALLY, PRESIDENT OBAMA UTTERS THAT FREIGHTED, OIL-DRENCHED WORD: *SPECULATION*

Posted: 03/08/2012, 8:07 AM EDT

At a press conference on March 6, 2012 when, lo and behold, while ruminating on the sky-high price of gasoline and the price of its core and price determinant raw material, crude oil, President Obama uttered that freighted word *speculation,* as in the following remarks: "So we're going to look at a whole range of measures— including, by the way, making sure that my Attorney General is paying attention to potential speculation in the oil markets. I've asked him to reconstitute a task force that's examining that."[42]

This surprising aside while sermonizing us with the usual exculpatory rhetoric emanating from the White House that "what I have also said about gas prices is that there is no silver bullet ..." to high, ever-higher gasoline prices other than better mileage standards for new cars reaching 55 miles per gallon by 2025, and "we're going [to] develop clean energy technologies that allow us to continue to use less oil."[43]

All well and good, but it is the aside referring to speculation that holds the most immediate promise. But, then again, vesting Attorney General Eric Holder with that responsibility is perhaps not much better than letting the speculation-appeasing Commodity Futures Trading Commission (CFTC) check into the matter. Back in April 2011, Attorney General Holder was given the mandate to form the Oil and Gas Price Fraud Working Group. To date, no report, no findings, no indictments, and, as far as the public can tell, no follow-up.

If only President Obama would hoist the banner of that stalwart purveyor of bullets from our folk history and go after the oil boys and their speculator coconspirators the way they went after the bad guys in his day, faster than a speeding bullet. ...

Obama Fulminates Over China's Export Restrictions on Rare Earths While Silent on OPEC's Collusion

Posted: 03/18/2012, 7:19 PM EDT

Rare earth minerals are critical inputs in the manufacture of high-tech products, ranging from computers and mobile devices, to hybrid cars, and on to missiles. More than 95 percent of the world's rare earths are produced in China. China, in turn, has instituted rigid export quotas, as well as extensive taxes and export fees, all of which have contributed to significant price surges of rare earths in recent years.

Acting in tandem with the European Union (EU) and Japan, the president announced last week in Washington, "If China would simply let the market work on its own, we'd have no objections. But their policies currently are preventing that from happening ..."[44]

Ironically, the president's concerns about the workings of the market came almost in lockstep with a moment of vacuous hypocrisy, when the world's top oil producers, preparing to meet in Kuwait, voiced concern that high oil prices could jeopardize a global economic recovery, as though Kuwait, seat of one of the leading OPEC practitioners, and its fellow cabal adherents, could not have done much, much more to prevent oil prices from reaching their current extortionist levels. To make the markets even more nervous, after extensive assurances that they stood ready to fill any gap caused by the Iranian oil embargo, the Saudis took the occasion to begin backtracking on their solidarity with oil embargo policies toward Iran, when the Saudi official spokesman announced their reluctance to stay the course: "We don't want to replace Iranian oil, and we never said we wanted to. We will step in and fill any gap if needed."[45] He probably should have added, "If prices remain high enough."

So on it goes. OPEC continues to practice its collusionary restraint of trade, with nary a word of condemnation given the influence of oil interests, the commodity exchanges, and our incredibly oblivious courts, which, by extending sovereign immunity to OPEC's national oil companies, permit them to manipulate shamelessly. This manipulation thereby ratchets up oil prices to the enormous benefit of the oil companies who are reporting record-breaking profits, at a staggering cost to the public in the form of gasoline, diesel, and heating oil prices, all the while placing the health of the economy in danger.

Given President Obama's sudden concern for letting the "market work on its own," perhaps it's time to revisit the efforts made during the Bush administration to pass No Oil Producing Exporting Cartels (NOPEC) legislation, which would have permitted the Department of Justice (DOJ) and the Federal Trade Commission (FTC) to sue OPEC under US antitrust laws. In 2007, the Senate (70–23) and the House (345–72) voted overwhelmingly for the NOPEC bill, permitting legal action against the national oil companies of the oil cartel. [46] Not generally understood is OPEC's ability to operate outside the law, hiding behind our sovereign immunity shield in such a way that has enabled the oil companies and oil interests to have benefited in the billions, if not trillions, over the years. [Please see "Oil: A Defining Moment for Our Political Class and the Press," *Huffington Post* (blog), July 9, 2007.[47]]

To judge the merits of the bill by its detractors, one need only to have looked as far as the American Petroleum Institute, the trade association of the oil industry, and such Washington Beltway think tanks as the Energy Policy Research Foundation, in part funded by the oil industry,[48] whose director, Larry Goldstein, at the time was quoted as saying, "Our friends in the Middle East understand we are just venting steam." Most significant was then president of the United States George W. Bush's clear threat, given his ties to the oil industry and Saudi interests, to veto the legislation should it have landed on his desk.

But that was then and now is now. In the near four years of President Obama's administration virtually nothing has been done to slow or reverse the steep escalation of oil, and, in turn, gasoline prices. Almost from the inception of his administration, the price of oil ballooned from $33/barrel in February 2009 to over $105/barrel today. Certainly refocusing government's attention on No Oil Producing Exporting Cartels (NOPEC), a law that might have helped enormously to restrain prices. Given the government's silence on this issue, its general lack of initiative on matters directly impacting oil prices—be it OPEC or commodity speculation—one begins to wonder if, on the issues of oil and its price, President Obama has become an acolyte of former president George W. Bush.

If restraint of trade in matters relating to China's control and manipulation of the rare earths market is of current and pressing concern, then focus on the OPEC oil cartel and its impact on the price of oil and gasoline, on our economy and national security, is long past due, certainly, and, at the very least, for the number of years that this administration has been in office. It is well past time that our government acts on behalf of the national interest rather the moneyed influence of the oil companies and their allies.

Obama's "All-of-the-Above" Oil/ Energy Policy Misguidedly Leaves Much off the Table

Posted: 03/25/2012, 2:43 PM EDT

On March 22, in Cushing, Oklahoma—a municipality key to the nation's oil and gas industry, as it represents the cited location for domestic crude oil deliveries and is central to the determination of the WTI (West Texas Intermediate) crude oil price quoted on the commodity exchanges—President Obama, while rationalizing his holding back approval of the full Keystone XL pipeline project because of environmental concerns, assured his audience that the southern leg of the Keystone route, from Cushing, Oklahoma, to the Gulf Coast, would become "a priority."

Well, thank you, Mr. President. Without the flow-through originating in Alberta, Keystone's point of origin, you will be helping to increase the price of oil by some $20/barrel. You see, Cushing is choking with oil; its storage capacity is filled to the rafters from the new shale oil wells in North Dakota, Wyoming, and so on. It has brought the price of US quoted crude oil to a discount of some $20/barrel, compared to that of the quoted price of Brent crude (Brent $125.13/barrel versus WTI 106.87/barrel). With the new pipeline in place, and without the back up of Alberta oil, that difference will all but disappear, and we will all be paying higher prices for gasoline.

But isn't that the objective your secretary of energy, Steven Chu, has received the mandate to achieve? Before a congressional hearing on February 29, 2012, Secretary Chu was asked by Representative Alan Nunnelee (R-MS) if the "overall goal is to get our price [of gasoline down] ..." But he didn't finish his question, because Chu interrupted him with, "No, the overall goal is to decrease our dependency on oil."[49] This coming from the Nobel Prize winner whom the *Wall Street Journal* quoted as saying, "Somehow we have to figure out how to boost the price of gasoline to the levels in Europe."[50]

As President Obama stated in his talk, "The price of oil will be set by the global market."[51] He then went on to instruct us, "and that means every time there's tensions that rise in the Middle East—which is what's happening right now—so will the price of gas—the reason that gas prices are high right now is because people are worried about what's happening in Iran ... if something happens there could be trouble, and so were going to price oil higher just in case."

They must be popping champagne corks on the commodity exchange floors all over the world. Here is the president of the United States validating one of the biggest canards used to explain away the extortionist level of oil prices. Not a word about excessive speculation or even manipulation. The exchanges can now rest easy, as we can now forget about the testimony proffered by Rex Tillerson, chairman and CEO of the world's largest publicly traded oil company, ExxonMobil, who stated in Senate hearings in May 2011, that $30 to $40 of the $100/barrel oil trading at that time, was the result of speculation. And, only recently, the St. Louis Federal Reserve released its pointed study on the impact of speculation on oil prices, *Speculation in the Oil Market*, which, with profound intelligence, begins its study with the admonishment, "Disentangling the true drivers of oil prices is a critical first step for allocating resources and designing good policy."[52]

Nor does the president give us any definition of what he means by "world market". "Markets" normally implies prices set by the marketplace; that is to say, by supply and demand. Yet again he is validating a process that is as far from the norms of a "free marketplace" as one could get.

First and foremost, the oil market is conditioned by a cartel acting in massive restraint of trade. To the extent that, were they American companies colluding, they would have been held to account by our Department of Justice (DOJ) and Federal Trade Commission (FTC) years ago. Yet this administration has done virtually nothing to break OPEC's death grip on the oil markets, not even bringing forth a No Oil Producing Exporting Cartels (NOPEC) statute that would have withdrawn the sovereign immunity exemption from the OPEC national oil companies, permitting the DOJ, et al., to institute legal proceedings.[53]

Nor has there been a serious effort to direct our lame oversight agencies, such as the Commodity Futures Trading Commission (CFTC), to finally get serious about reining in excessive speculation, both here and in concert with commodity exchanges around the world where transparency of any kind is lacking. Do we know, for example, whether Russian interests are playing the London crude oil markets in order to maneuver or manipulate the price of oil? Are they? Aren't they? I don't know. But the price of oil is critical to the well-being of the Russian economy to a degree that has enormous political and social ramifications.[54] Russia, of course, has become a major exporter of crude oil, at the level of Saudi Arabia. Russia is also the major supplier of natural gas to Europe, and, here again, the price "quoted" for oil is paramount. Russia's gas contracts with its European customer base are tied directly to the price of crude, which at today's Brent crude oil price results in gas prices north of $15.00/MMBtu, which leads to another issue, or lack thereof, in the president's lecture.

In citing his "all-of-the above" strategy toward "I want us to control our own energy destiny," the president refers to biofuels, to solar energy, to wind energy. Glaringly omitted is any reference (as though it was taboo) to our vast newly accessible resources of natural gas, enough to last us more than a hundred years, and we are but at the initial stages of this evolving game changer. With natural gas, we have a market made up of producers all within the United States. Any collusion would be immediately slapped down by the antitrust vigilantes—meaning that we really have a "market," where supply and demand determine price without all the attendant game playing. What does that really mean?

In Europe, with its lack of transparency and its deeply vested interests, the price consumers of natural gas are paying is $15.00/MMBtu, plus. Here in the United States, with a plentiful supply and an unencumbered marketplace, the price is less than $2.50/MMBtu—an enormous difference! Even more telling, the price of crude, competing with natural gas at less than $2.50/MMBtu, would have to be priced at less than $20/barrel to deliver the same energy quotient. Not only is "our" (not an unimportant word in this context) natural gas vastly cheaper than crude oil as to the energy it delivers, but it is also much cleaner burning. What our president should have said is that this government is moving heaven and earth to convert our transportation fleet from gasoline and diesel to compressed natural gas (CNG) power. That all will be done to help Detroit retool, to help car owners either convert or trade-in, to set up an efficient and nationwide distribution system for CNG. Such a program would not only make us energy independent, it would also collapse the price of oil, which at current levels is not only endangering our economy, but, given the political antagonism of many of the societies that benefit from high oil prices, our national security as well.

The Price of Oil: Saudi Hypocrisy, Our Gullibility

Posted: 03/30/2012, 4:04AM EDT

We should feel compelled to pull out that old chestnut, "There he goes again." The face of Saudi oil, and the de facto senior voice of the OPEC cartel, Saudi oil minister Ali al-Naimi entertained us to one of his seminal dissertations, expounding on Saudi Arabia's concerns for the well-being of all mankind.[55]

Stating the case clearly, he asserted that Saudi Arabia "remains the world's largest producer and the country with the largest proven reserves, so it has a responsibility to do what it can to mitigate prices." No argument here. [Please see "Saudi Arabia Will Act to Lower Soaring Oil Prices," by Ali al-Naimi, *Financial Times*, March 28, 2012.]

Yet he prefaced that bit of wisdom with this, the oldest of canards: "Needless to say, Saudi Arabia does not control the price: it sells its crude according to international prices." A truly bizarre declaration coming from the leading protagonist of the cartel, OPEC, whose primary function is to limit the supply of oil to world markets, to control, and, within the limits of the world's tolerance, to maximize the price of crude oil in the marketplace. Clearly OPEC'S efforts

38

have been so successful that the limits of tolerance have now been reached, and letting off a little steam has become part of the ritual.

The ritual is encapsulated in the mantra repeated in Mr. Ali al-Naimi's pronouncement: "The bottom line is that Saudi Arabia would like to see a lower price. It would like to see a fair and reasonable price that will not hurt the economic recovery, especially in emerging and developing countries ..." A statement that automatically elicits our well-inculcated and -programmed hosannas whenever such mumblings come out of Riyadh.

The trouble is that we have heard this babble before. In December of 2008, with oil prices teetering below $40/and gasoline prices accordingly restrained, and, after King Abdullah himself had ventured that $75/barrel was a fair and reasonable price, our now benevolent Saudi oil minister Ali al-Naimi pontificated in order to enlighten us, "You must understand that the purpose of the $75 [per barrel] price is for a much more noble cause. You need every producer to produce, and marginal producers cannot produce at $40 a barrel."[56] This coming from a producer whose "all-inclusive" production costs veer toward $1.50/barrel, or possibly less, according to a pronouncement made by none other than Mr. Ali al-Naimi himself at the Houston Oil Forum in November 1999.[57]

Well, several months after the December 2008 statement giving us the parameters of oil price "nobility," the price touched and quickly breached Mr. Ali al-Naimi's $75/barrel. As it went shooting on to $100/barrel and well beyond, barely a word of discomfiture came from OPEC's headquarters or the Saudi oil ministry.

As the price veered to $100 and higher, the International Energy Agency was presumptive enough to criticize[58] OPEC for holding back production only to be roundly reprimanded by OPEC's

Secretary General el-Badri, who blamed high prices on speculation and "technical means," whatever that means.

Speaking of speculation—or worse, *manipulation*—and given the lack of transparency in the trading of oil futures in the world's commodity markets, it would be interesting to hear from Mr. Ali al-Naimi whether the Saudi oil ministry, Aramco, the Saudi Sovereign Wealth Fund, or whomever the Saudis or OPEC have designated, are currently holding oil futures contracts—and to what purpose. Certainly not to lower the price of oil!

Anyway, thank you, Mr. Ali al-Naimi. Your sincerity and good deeds are appreciated.

Shell Supports Iran's Murderous Mullahs; Should We Be Supporting Shell?

Posted: 04/02/2012, 5:16 AM EDT

The callous greed in the oil patch seems to know no limits. Here we have a company, Royal Dutch Shell (a.k.a, Shell Oil), bursting with earnings and at the apogee of its yearly returns, but going after the last dollar or euro to make things fatter still. This to the cold dismissal of the brave Iranians who rose en masse in 2009 to rally for free elections, only to be put down brutally by the mullahs' goon squads, financed in large measure by the plenitude of oil revenues streaming from Iran's export oil loadings. The world was outraged, but helplessly stood by as the slaughter continued. From far and wide came calls to impose sanctions on Iran and to impose embargoes on Iran's products. One would have thought any responsible organization would have desisted its activities with what had now evolved into a murderous regime.

Clearly conscious of the public outrage that would result from its moral turpitude continuing to enrich the mullahs, Shell did all it could to hide its transactional baseness with the Iranian dictatorship. For example, in March 2010, the *Wall Street Journal* reported that the tanker *Front Page* left the port of Fujairah, UAE, to sail on to Saudi Arabia.[59]

All well and good. But wait, tracking information revealed a very different course. The *Front Page* made an unreported stop along the coast of Iran to load a cargo of Iranian oil. Who was the charterer of this brazen attempt to hide its continuing "business as usual" with an Iranian government in the midst of imposing draconian oppression on its people? Yes, Shell Oil.

Since that time very little has changed, other than to become more grotesque. Shell's gorging on Iranian oil continued ongoing. Just this past week, Reuters reported, "Shell Scrambles to Pay Huge Bill for Iran Oil."[60]

We learned that Shell is struggling to pay off $1 billion that it owes the National Iranian Oil Company (NIOC), the equivalent of about eight million barrels of oil. Apparently, Shell has become Iran's second biggest oil buyer, having been outdistanced only by France's Total, which, however, ceased its Iranian oil purchases at the end of last year.

But it seems Shell toils on, now having to navigate through the labyrinth of financial sanctions in order to placate its Iranian pushers. And, as the Reuters report would have it, "Shell is working hard to figure out a way to pay NIOC."

All of which, of course, raises this question: given Shell's willingness to help sustain the murderous Iranian regime, should we as consumers exercise our individual initiative in solidarity with the oppressed people of Iran? (Remember the deeply poignant death of Nedā Āghā-Soltān on the streets of Tehran on June 20, 2009.[61]) In our daily lives, perhaps it is now necessary to decide where, and from whom, we buy our gasoline!

Oh yes, by the way, another point of focus. Should we be comfortable with the imminent ruling that our government agencies, especially the US Department of the Interior, are about to make that would permit Royal Dutch Shell to drill off Alaska's Beaufort and Chuckchi Seas? Should we vest that responsibility with a corporation of such vacuous concern?

THE NEW YORK TIMES SHEDS A TEAR FOR WALL STREET PAYDAYS

Posted: 04/08/2012, 4:19 PM EDT

Andrew Ross Sorkin, the *New York Time* columnist and CNBC talking head, a stealth apologist for Wall Street, Goldman Sachs, et al., slinks again[62]—this time in a featured babble on the growing difficulties encountered by the Wall Street folk to strike it big time.[63]

Mr. Sorkin presents us with a laundry list of why the cascade of wealth showered on Wall Street players is coming to an end. That henceforward times are going to be tough, with the implication that we should all be more charitable and understanding in our judgments of the errant behavior that has done so much to bring our economy close to its knees. He plaintively intones, "It is harder than ever to become one of the world's wealthiest individuals by working on Wall Street."

He then goes on to draw a distinction between the Wall Street pooh-bahs, such as JPMorgan Chase's Jamie Dimon and Goldman Sachs's Lloyd Blankfein, describing them as the poorer cousins of the hedge-fund crowd. This is a bit like saying they all belly-up to the same bar, but one set is drinking scotch while the other is ordering gin.

Then he continues, brimming with a subtext of the unfairness of it all, that the Wall Street types haven't reached the lofty heights of wealth, such as the likes of a Bill Gates. Without any qualifier, he thereby implies that Bill Gates's billions were achieved by means of the same razzle-dazzle as the Wall Street players and their speculative excesses. He in no way mentions that Bill Gates earned his billions by his exemplar of American meritocracy, thanks to his entrepreneurial vision and courage—through which we have all realized richer lives. Gates's path to the pinnacle of wealth stands in stark contrast to the largely self-enriching crony capitalism of Wall Street laid bare by the events of 2008 and thereafter.

In the meantime, working in the trenches, getting their hands dirty on farms, on assembly lines, tending the sick in emergency rooms, driving the trucks or buses, getting splattered with oil working on a rig, or whatever day-to-day undertakings in which they were engaged, clearly those below were too busy to take heed of Mr. Sorkin's concerns. Last year alone these hardworking souls pulled in the following paydays from one year's sweat and labor: [64]

> Ray Dalio, Bridgewater Associates, $3.9 billion
> Carl Icahn, Icahn Capital Management, $2.5 billion
> James H. Simmons, Renaissance Technologies Corp, $2.1 billion
> Kenneth C. Griffin, Citadel, $700 million
> Steven A. Cohen, SAC Capital Partners, $585 million

If timing is everything, then the timing of Mr. Sorkin's article becomes ever so curious, coming just one week after the publication of these humungous sums. There he was, as so often before, trying to steer our focus from the excesses of Wall Street's "big money parade.

Secretary of Energy Chu, and the Price You Are Paying for Gasoline

Posted: 04/16/2012, 8:39 AM EDT

What a day! Last Wednesday, those of us who could shell out the price of fifteen barrels of crude oil were treated to a plethora of oil industry canned (barreled?) wisdom on oil and energy, its present and future, by a battery of veterans and experts in the field, from that sly and wizened old fox T. Boone Pickens to Nobel Prize winner Steven Chu, at the *New York Times* Energy for Tomorrow conference sponsored by the *New York Times* (April 11, 2012).

Much was learned; much was overlooked. In its introductory handout, that day's Energy special section of the *New York Times*, the tone was set by the *Times* indefatigable oil reporter Jad Mouawad, who, in his featured reportage instructed us all, the great unwashed, that "oil is a global commodity whose price is set on the global market."[65] Here was the gospel of oil patch doctrine—complete with its inference that it' all about "supply and demand" when setting prices on the world market. Not a whisper about that force of nature, the OPEC oil cartel, nor the massive distortion rendered by the hundreds of billions of barrels of oil traded and the speculation inherent in world commodity exchanges.

Perhaps the highlight of the day's presentations was the conversation held with our current secretary of energy, Dr. Steven Chu, who was quoted in the *Wall Street Journal* in 2008 as saying, "Somehow we have to boost the price of gasoline to the levels in Europe,"[66] and his interlocutor, columnist Tom Friedman. The very same Dr. Chu was told earlier in March by Representative Alan Nunnelee (R-MS): "I can't look at motivations. I have to look at results. And under this administration, the price of gasoline has doubled. ... The people of north Mississippi can't be here, so I have to be here and be their voice for them. ... I have to tell you that $8-a-gallon gasoline makes them afraid. It's a cruel tax on the people of north Mississippi as they try to go back and forth to work. It's a cloud hanging over economic development and job creation."[67] Chu expressed sympathy but said his department "is working to lower energy prices in the long term." There now, does that make you feel warm and cozy up in Maine?

And so the conversation went, as though the here and now had nothing to do with the secretary of energy's concerns. The price we are all paying at the pump or for heating oil is too mundane to be touched upon by Dr. Chu. It's a bit like having to leave the aerie of the ivy-covered walls of academe and get your hands dirty on an oilrig.

Confronted with questions about the Solyndra debacle that cost the government more than $500 million in failed, clearly botched guarantees, Dr. Chu interjected that Congress had set aside some $10 billion for potentially failed energy investments, as if to imply that calling him to account for a mere $500 million was not quite in line. "It is what it is," we were told.

During the entire interview, not a word about the issue on the minds of most Americans: the price they are paying at the pump. As though this was outside the purview of the Department of Energy (DOE). But see it all for yourself: nytenergyfortomorrow[68] on livestream.com.

President Obama Speaks, and the Oil Speculators React

Posted: 04/24/2012, 7:28 AM EDT

Last week President Obama gave the nation a briefing from the White House on the perils of speculation and the potential for abuse in oil futures trading, contributing to the distortion of oil prices and in turn the high price for gasoline we are paying at the pump.[69] Though short on specifics, the president did call for increasing penalties, both civil and criminal, for market manipulation and significantly increasing the budget of the oversight agencies, such as the Commodity Futures Trading Commission (CFTC), so as to "crack down on illegal activity and hold accountable those who manipulate the market for private gain at the expense of millions of working families."

Promptly, of course, as if on cue, from its headquarters in Chicago's Loop, the prodigious exchange operator, the CME Group, the largest in the country, comprising the Chicago Mercantile Exchange (CME), the Chicago Board of Trade (CBOT), the New York Mercantile Exchange (NYMEX, where oil futures contracts are traded), and the Commodity Exchange, Inc. (COMEX), called the president's plan "misplaced".[70]

Wall Street, in the mantle of a Citigroup head of commodities research, immediately opined, according to CNBC's dutifully entitled "Obama's Plan Could Increase Price Swings" (April 20, 12), and reported in writing by Reuters, "The attack on speculation is an attack on better functioning markets. If there were not liquidity in the futures market ... the chances are overwhelming that price volatility would be greater."[71]

There's no knowledge or appreciation here of the sage words uttered before the Senate Committee on Government Affairs as long ago as November 1, 1990 by Leon Hess, the founder and chairman of Hess Oil: "I'm an old man, but I'd bet my life if the Merc [New York Mercantile Exchange] was not in operation, there would be ample oil at reasonable prices all over the world without this volatility."[72] Clearly, some words of wisdom only become wiser with time.

Consider the distortion the futures markets bring to oil trading. In 2011, the average daily volume on the NYMEX was just under 190,000 contracts per day, shooting up to an all-time high of 311,000 during the Libyan cutoff in February/March 2011, when prices rose to a yearly peak of $110.55/barrel for West Texas Intermediate (WTI).

Each futures contract is for 1,000 barrels of oil. At 190,000 contracts/ day, that represents 190 million barrels of oil traded daily on the NYMEX alone, not to mention the exchanges in London, Singapore, Dubai, Hong Kong, and so on, who cumulatively far exceed trading on the NYMEX. Now the daily consumption worldwide of actual "wet barrels" of crude oil is some 85 million barrels/day. One would be hard-pressed to present a coherent economic justification for the enormous difference between the vast number of derivative, or "paper barrels," traded on the exchanges versus the number of "wet barrels" actually shipped and consumed.

And then, as if preprogrammed, in the very same week that the CFTC announced a "milestone victory" in its first major case against algorithmic oil trading, as well as the biggest financial penalty involving manipulation in the oil futures markets.[73] The CFTC alleged that the Dutch firm Optiver's Chicago office attempted to move US crude, gasoline, and heating oil prices by executing large volume trades during the final moments of trading as the exchanges settled their end-of-trading-day prices. The court decreed that Optiver was to pay $14 million: $1 million in disgorged profits and $13 million in fines.

"Those who seek to manipulate oil or other commodity markets should know we aren't messing around," Bart Chilton, certainly the most attuned CFTC Commissioner, was quoted as saying. [74] Yes, but this case dates back to 2007, and its prosecution shows how sclerotic the process is and how ineffectual oversight has become in the tsunami of commodity trading of oil and oil products worldwide. Where there is no cop on the beat, anything goes, and with an ineffectual cop, almost anything. As if to assuage the trading community in the face of this "milestone" victory, and seemingly forever responsive to the relentless lobbying by such as the commodity exchanges and the bank holding companies, the CFTC, in its inimical fashion of oversight mandate monitoring of derivatives trading, last week significantly narrowed the range of companies that were to be subject to rigid requirements and heightened supervision.

Frequently, the current price of natural gas at under $2.00/MMBtu, trading at ten-year lows, is given as proof positive of the effectiveness of the commodity markets.

Or, as Reuters quoted, "that while politicians had been quick to criticize speculators in oil, they've been quiet about speculators in the natural gas market, who have been betting on lower gas prices since at least June 2009, according data from the CFTC."[75]

Perhaps this is so, but as currently traded on the US exchanges, natural gas is exclusively sourced in the United States, without the interface of such collusionary price distortions as those orchestrated by OPEC, and also without the opaque trading over commodity exchanges worldwide, open to all manner of influences. Natural gas, as traded today on US exchanges, is a uniquely isolated American commodity, and any attempt to influence its price, overt or otherwise, would fall under the purview of the nation's antitrust laws and stated prohibitions to all manner of collusion. Ergo, the cop on the beat goes well beyond the lame CFTC, but in this instance, also includes the Department of Justice (DOJ) and the Federal Trade Commission (FTC). In other words, enough firepower to make sure the playing field remains an honest playing field and a true reflection of supply and demand. In effect, the price of natural gas as traded here serves as a beacon to highlight the enormous distortion in the traded price of crude oil.

T. Boone Pickens Dances the Saudi Oil Polka

Posted: 05/02/2012, 7:59 AM EDT

There he was on CNBC, of course, the man most identified with and heralded as the ultimate oil guru: T. Boone Pickens, interviewed by Maria Bartiromo on April 30.[76] Being the conscientious reporter that she is, amidst Pickens's musings on natural gas and other vistas of the oil/energy patch, Bartiromo quite naturally asked Mr. Pickens where oil prices were heading.

Well, they were headed up, said the man, and then he explained, well, you see the Saudis are "maxed out". They can't produce more. And there in one fell swoop, he gave the Saudis a free pass on the current oil price distortions and turned the Saudis from the OPEC cabal's malevolent gorgon into our heroic good guys, doing all they can to pump away, trying to come up with as much oil as they can, but unable to meet our ravenous appetite to thereby keep oil prices in check. This is totally in line with the propaganda line that Saudis pump their capacity full-out, but they can only do so much. So please pay and don't complain, and the more you pay the better off we (the Saudis) and Mr. Pickens's oil investments will be.

As knowledgeable as he is purported to be on oil matters and, now, seemingly, on Saudi oil issues, Mr. Pickens fails to remind us (or the Saudis, of course), of the study Aramco, Saudi Arabia's state-owned national oil behemoth, fashioned in the 1970s. It was a comprehensive plan calling for Saudi Arabia to increase its production capacity to twenty million barrels/day by the 1990s. (Today, in 2012, it is purported to be twelve million barrels/day). One wonders what happened to that study, which was widely heralded at the time and envisaged as a safety net for a massively burgeoning oil-consuming world economy.

Nor in assuring us of Saudi Arabia's heroic efforts and good works did Mr. Pickens make any reference to the crafted distortion of what is accepted wisdom of Saudi national oil reserves at some 260 billion barrels. [77]

This in spite of a revelationary first page article that appeared in the *New York Times* on March 5, 2007, "New Innovations Pumping New Life into Old Wells," whereby Nansen G. Saleri, head of reservoir management of Aramco, said that he estimated, with new drilling technologies, that potential reserves were three times the officially published figure of 260 billion barrels. [78] The estimate he gave then was 716 billion barrels, and he added he "wouldn't be surprised" if ultimate resources reached 1 trillion barrels. The new technology has, over the last few years, vastly expanded the oil and gas reserves of the United States. One can only imagine what its prospects are for Saudi Arabia.

In closing, to make us feel better, Mr. Pickens ventured that we in the United States are fortunate to have the lowest oil and gas prices in the world. It seems that if and when Mr. Pickens visits his friends in Saudi Arabia, he is chauffeured and comes into no contact with a gasoline pump where gas is selling for some $0.61 per gallon. [79]

Oh yes, it is understood Mr. Pickens has had almost open access to the White House. Could there be a correlation to the energy mess we are living in now? [80]

Blatant Insider Commodity Trading Given Pass That Would Put Stock Traders in Handcuffs

Posted: 05/06/2012, 11:49 AM EDT

Quite incredible, as reported last week in the *New York Times*, which quotes Reuters: Aubrey K. McClendon, while acting as Chesapeake Energy chairman and CEO, had run a "hedge fund that traded commodities, including natural gas futures, for at least four years while he led Chesapeake's vast expansion of gas drilling" and oversaw both companies' hedging activities in oil and gas futures.[81] The $200 million fund, Heritage Management Company, used Chesapeake's Oklahoma City headquarters as its mailing address.

Certainly nice work if you can get it. And that's the rub, according to our heavily lobbied commodity exchanges and Wall Street–influenced law: commodity trading is more loosely regulated than equity markets. The article picked up from Reuters quoted Morningstar analyst Mark Hanson as saying this in reference to McClendon's catbird seat at the gaming table: "If he knows Chesapeake is to ramp up or curtail production, he could enter into positions in his hedge funds that could benefit from that." Had it been the stocks and bonds of his company trading on insider information, the SEC would have made an appearance bearing handcuffs. [82]

Here we have this enormous dichotomy between insider trading in stocks and bonds, and commodities. The difference is simply this: with commodity trading, most everyone is impacted. Insider trading in oil and gas always trickles down to the public as Chevron showed83 us when its traders held oil and product contracts for twenty-seven million barrels of oil and trading profits for the first seven months of 2011, cashing in over $260 million at the public's expense. Remember, these twenty-seven million barrels were not for producing and selling, but for trading alone; the $260 million in profits came strictly from trades, and we can well assume that these actions were not meant to push prices of Chevron's core products down. Thus, those trading profits were underwritten by the rest of us in the form of higher prices for gasoline, heating oil, and diesel.

As I said, it's nice work if you can get it. And it is long overdue that commodities trading oversight and regulation be put on the same playing field as trading in stocks and bonds, with the same level of enforcement—both civil and criminal—that applies to insider trading under our securities laws.

JPMorgan's $2 Billion Loss, and the Price You Are Paying for Gas at the Pump

Posted: 05/11/2012, 10:40 AM EDT

JPMorgan is a bank holding company. Under current law that means it not only functions as a bank but also as a casino. The process begins with easy and practically cost-free money, to which JPMorgan has access at the Federal Reserve under its guise as a bank, but then it uses that money to play roulette by betting on derivatives and commodities, such as copper, crude oil, petroleum products, financial derivatives, and so on. [Please see "JPMorgan Chase Banks on Buying into the Casino," *Huffington Post* (blog), November 25, 2011.[84]]

We could readily hypothesize that the recent spike in oil prices resulted in part from JPMorgan bets[85] that the price of oil would go higher, which, in effect, pushed up the price of oil, and, consequently, the price of gasoline. JPMorgan is a "bank" that has chartered oil tankers with the capacity of tens of thousands, if not hundreds of thousands, of tons, filled them with millions of barrels of crude oil and petroleum products, and kept them at anchor at sea for months at a time in order to game the price of oil. Of course, when one buys oil, takes it off the market, and loads it on tankers for speculation, the price doesn't go down; the price goes up, and we all end up bankrolling JPMorgan's casino gambit by paying higher prices for gas at the pump. All this while the Fed pumps more and more money into JPMorgan, permitting it to buy more and more oil at bargain-basement cost, a financing bargain gambit not available to refineries and those who actually *use* the oil and could pass along those economies to consumers.

The price of oil has been going down the last couple of weeks. Is it because (or at least in part because) JPMorgan has had to vacate its long oil positions? If so, will the Fed now step in and give JPMorgan the additional liquidity it needs to salvage its positions, at our cost, by pushing up the traded price of oil futures? This will result in higher prices at the pump fashioned by the Fed's "help" in supporting JPMorgan, and it will all be at our expense. If this happens, the Fed's mandate needs a massive overhaul, and our government needs to refocus its priorities from bailing Wall Street out of the mess they have gotten all of us into, and, instead, focusing on how bailing out Wall Street plays out on Main Street.

The *Wall Street Journal's* Convoluted Whitewash of Jamie Dimon

Posted: 05/14/2012, 6:56PM EDT

One of the most convoluted, opaque editorials ("The Dimon Principle"[86]) that the *Wall Street Journal* has been able to muster appeared today. Alluding to JPMorgan Chase's $2 billion trading loss, it opened with the following hosanna to Jamie Dimon, and delivered a slap on the wrist to those in government and elsewhere who now feel that Dimon's aggressive proprietary trading policies have finally come home to roost: "Employees at JPMorgan may think that CEO Jamie Dimon's primary rule is to minimize risk. But Washington politicians now have their own Dimon Principle: use mistakes at a bank run by an admired CEO to expand government control over financial markets."

The editorial goes on breathlessly in technical hodgepodge jargon, with nary a mention of the obdurate and relentless policies initiated by Dimon in order to turn JPMorgan Chase into a casino on a scale barely known or countenanced before. There was the eye-opening broad exposé in the very same *Wall Street Journal's* October 2010 article, "JPMorgan's Commodities Chief Takes the Heat"[87]. [Please also see "Bravo JPMorgan! Just What We Need, Another Wall Street Casino," October 12, 2010.[88]] The article details JPMorgan's full court press ambitions "to build the number-one commodities trading franchise on the planet." Barely deterred by the events of 2008, JPMorgan was busy doing the following:

- spending then $2 billion acquiring the trading assets of Bear Stearns and UBS Commodities in 2008, and the Royal Bank of Scotland (RBS)'s Sempra Commodities in 2010

- poaching traders and executives from rivals

- boosting its trading workforce from some 125 in 2006 to 1,800 by October 2010

But building the casino wasn't enough for Dimon. A little over a year later, JPMorgan Chase took steps to buy the casino itself, acquiring a stake from that heralded provenance, MF Global, in the London Metal Exchange (LME), to make it the largest single shareholder. [Please see "JPMorgan Chase Banks on Buying into The Casino," *Huffington Post* (blog), November 25, 2011.[89]] At the time the *Telegraph* revealed that JPMorgan Chase was the "mystery trader" that bought £1 billion worth of copper on the LME. That purchase, according to the *Telegraph*, pushed up the price of copper to the highest level since the banking crisis in October 2008. Now that's banking as it should be!

And the beat went on. On Sunday, May 13, Mr. Dimon offered this telling prelude on NBC's *Meet the Press*: "There's almost no excuse for it."

Bloomberg reported in April of this year that JPMorgan's treasury and chief investment office held a combined $355.6 billion portfolio of investment securities as of December 2011.[90] At the time, the now-departing chief investment officer, Ina Drew, was among

JPMorgan's highest-paid executives in 2011, earning $14 million. Her imminent departure from JPMorgan resulted, we can only assume, largely from the $2 billion-and-counting debacle.

Yet it would appear Ms. Drew was simply—or complexly—following the guidelines laid down over the years by the corner office, where banking had become second fiddle to the siren call of the roulette wheel.

Clearly, at JPMorgan Chase, the buck stops elsewhere.

Does JPMorgan's Derivatives Fiasco Portend the Collapse of Crude Oil and Gasoline Prices?

Posted: 05/21/2012, 8:33 AM EDT

According to the *Wall Street Journal*, JPMorgan's losses on what has been reported[91] as big directional bets on credit derivatives, but never fully disclosed by JPMorgan, could reach $5 billion or more. Along with credit derivatives and other commodities, such as copper, JPMorgan Chase is a behemoth trader in crude oil and petroleum products, both as physical product and its financial derivatives. Since April, the price of West Texas Intermediate (WTI) crude on the commodity exchanges has eroded, for a plethora of reasons, by some 14 percent a barrel, from near $105/barrel to just over $91/barrel, a massive decline in short order.

Now, I do not know JPMorgan's current oil trading book, nor do I know the positions it holds in physical crude oil and derivative futures contracts. But past history shows that JPMorgan is a major player risking hundreds of millions, if not billions, in oil trading positions. JPMorgan has a history not only of massive trading in oil futures but also taking title to enormous volumes of physical product held in shore storage and chartered VLCCs, which it leaves sitting for months at a time at anchor at sea. (VLCCs, or very large crude carriers, are enormous tankers able to hold more than two hundred thousand tons of cargo, some three times the size of the HMS *Queen Mary*.)

Given past trading practices, JPMorgan may be holding speculative cargoes of crude oil valued in the hundreds of millions of dollars. (Each ton contains 7.4 barrels of crude, multiplied by 200,000 tons purchased, say, at the hypothetical level of the recent price of $105/barrel, would value such a cargo at $155,400,000. This compared to a current price [close of trading Friday, May 18] of $91/barrel or $134,680,000, plus per diem chartering and holding charges, resulting in a paper loss of at least $20,720,000.) The parenthetical amounts are significant sums of money, but without the current credit derivatives imbroglio, it could well have been handled with equanimity by JPMorgan Chase. But that is the point, given the building losses in its other trading operations, JPMorgan may not reasonably be able to tolerate further deterioration in value of its proprietary commodity trading positions, and we could venture that the pressure to liquidate such positions is mounting, especially as prices erode. The question becomes, how large are JPMorgan's crude oil physical and derivative positions, and how much pressure is JPMorgan now under to liquidate?

JPMorgan has been a major player in pushing up the price of oil because of the speculative position the company takes, and these price hikes have played out "at the pump," so to speak. In other words, we are all paying for it in the price of gasoline. Perhaps this is the turnaround moment, and JPMorgan's current travails in trading will lead to lower gas prices. Please remember the previously cited testimony given by Rex Tillerson[92], chairman and CEO of ExxonMobil. If ever a personage should know, he should, and just a year ago, speaking before the Senate Finance Committee, Tillerson said that the then quoted price of $100/barrel incorporated $30 to $40/barrel attributable to speculation.

JPMorgan was not mentioned at that time, but when it comes to oil speculation, JPMorgan is among the leaders of the pack. [Please also see "Are Our Leaders Hearing ExxonMobil CEO Tillerson?," May 17, 2011.]

One further point: JPMorgan, as a supposed bank holding company, has ready access to the Federal Reserve cash window and its diminutive interest rates; in other words, taxpayer money. This, while simultaneously holding Federal Deposit Insurance Corporation (FDIC) secured deposits for which the government is the backstop of last resort. Thus, taxpayers are helping JPMorgan Chase run up the price of oil and gasoline at little cost to JPMorgan and to its enormous profit (and at the public's expense). Yet should all the trades blow up and the bank collapse, the government is left holding the tab. All the while we pay for it *a second time* in the form of elevated prices for gasoline at the pump.

Last is the irony of ironies: this cozy relationship with the Federal Reserve is memorialized by JPMorgan Chase bank chairman and CEO Jamie Dimon sitting on the board of the New York Federal Reserve (JPMorgan's piggy bank). It is a grotesque symbol of how the Wall Street banks control our government.

Mr. Dimon, sir, out of respect to our waning confidence in government institutions, your resignation from the Fed board is well past due.

Sheila Bair as Vice President. Governor Romney, Are You Listening?

Posted: 05/28/2012, 5:51 AM EDT

Wall Street, the financial sector, and its minions have much to answer for in their self-absorbed destabilization of the American economy now playing out in the crumbling lifestyles of so many Americans. This occurs while our government's largesse continues, through Washington-sponsored programs, such as the Troubled Asset Relief Program (TARP), ready liquidity at the Federal Reserve discount window, government-guaranteed bank deposits, a paucity of oversight of the stock and commodity exchanges, total absence of criminal prosecutions, and more—all doled out to the very perpetrators of America's economic malaise.

The issue defines itself with particular grimness in the putative candidates on our political stage. We have a president with a lack of understanding or volition to take on the power and influence of the financial industry, surrounding himself with appointees with deep ties to the culture of Wall Street, and, consequently, unwilling or unable to rein in its excesses. It has become an administration unwilling or unable to respond to the anger felt throughout the land, to the extent that "crony capitalism" has been permitted to flourish. In its stead, President Obama, unable to deal with distortions visited on the nation by the financial sector, has dangerously uncorked the two demons that have devastated so much of European history: class war and envy, proclivities that, in large dimensions, have been thankfully absent from the American psyche.

Governor Romney, in turn, is identified hand and fist with Wall Street's interests—whether because of his previous position as CEO of Bain Capital or his opposition to Dodd-Frank. In the case of the former, his past leadership of Bain Capital and the financial engineering it represents, remind us of all the leveraged buyouts that enrich the investors while saddling functioning businesses with enormous debt, ultimately destroying many, as well as all the resultant societal devastation of lost jobs, ruined careers, and hollowed townscapes such financial machinations portend. In the case of the former, his opposition to, and calls for repeal of, the Dodd-Frank Act, the one piece of legislation put forward by Congress to bridle the runaway power of the financial sector, even though as a bill it received such massive lobbying as to have approached near meaninglessness.

Yet it is still early in the campaign, and perhaps wisdom, with a little bit of luck, will yet fall on fertile ground. Despite Governor Romney's identification with a financial sector that has run roughshod over the nation and practically brought the nation's economy to its knees, redemption is still possible. It would be a coup of extraordinary dimension were his campaign to look to that singular personage in government who, from the very beginning of the financial imbroglio, fought tooth and nail for the interests of everyday America and against the untrammeled clout and billions doled out to the financial pooh-bahs of Wall Street and beyond. This was Sheila Bair, the erstwhile chair (June 2006–July 2011) of the Federal Deposit Insurance Corporation (FDIC). Bair, a moderate Republican and holdover appointee from the Bush administration, fought unstintingly against the crony capitalism that had overtaken our government. [Please see "America Needs a President Who Will Confront the Financial Industry's Hegemony Over Our Lives," *Huffington Post* (blog), July 14, 2011.[93]] "Our job is to protect bank customers, not banks," was her modus operandi. Just last week, Sheila Bair was extensively interviewed on CNBC by Maria Bartiromo, following Bair's public contention that, given its massive speculative losses, banks the size of JPMorgan Chase should be broken up, as their size is such that the market can no longer get a handle on them, the regulators cannot get a handle on them, and now, it's become clear, neither can their management. [But see for yourself: "Sheila Bair: Break Up JPMorgan," CNBC, Friday, May 25, 2012.[94]]

America needs a real choice this November. Governor Romney, are you listening?

COMMODITY EXCHANGES PRIME THE PUMP FOR HIGHER OIL/GASOLINE PRICES

Posted: 05/31/2012, 9:10 AM EDT

In April, the CME Group, the largest commodity exchange group in the country, blasted[95] the president's plan to put regulators in charge of margin requirements for oil futures, warning that the move risked raising prices. (The Chicago Mercantile Exchange (CME), the Chicago Board of Trade (CBOT), the New York Mercantile Exchange (NYMEX), and the Commodity Exchange, Inc. (COMEX) comprise the CME Group.)

The CME went on to pontificate, "The administration's proposal to use margin requirements to control cash prices is misplaced. Taking away from the exchanges the ability to manage margins would make the markets less efficient, less tied to fundamentals, and would create the potential to push the hedges out of the market, which would make oil more expensive for all consumers."

Really!?

There is a large body of discourse[96] pointing to the untrammeled, barely regulated trading on the exchanges, which has distorted the price of crude oil and in turn oil products, such as gasoline, causing such prices to rise ever higher, losing all vestiges of any connection to supply and demand. The commodity exchanges have become casinos: they welcome all players whose only interest is the spin of the roulette wheel, never consuming, producing, or taking title to the oil they are placing bets on. As far as the exchanges go, their key concern is to keep the players coming in the door.

This might all seem well and good, but the croupier begins to play a far more sinister role when he not only provides the gaming table but also manipulates the price of the gaming chips. Over the past weeks, we have seen a significant break in oil prices. Here, for once in months, if not years, we have an oil market evolving in a way that could significantly reduce oil and gasoline prices, and, in turn, put a damper on the hectic tempo of oil trading on the exchanges—it seems lower prices result in lower exchange turnover. So to give some underpinning to sliding oil prices, it would appear that the CME Group, knowing where its collective bread is buttered, did what it could in order to bring in more traders and trades in what could be seen as an attempt to support the eroding price of oil/gasoline. To wit, the CME Group lowered the margin requirements for each crude oil contract of one thousand barrels from $6,885 per contract to $6,210, making it that much less expensive to buy your chips, so more can play in the casino to help halt the slippage of crude/gasoline prices.

Maybe we should all send our next gas station tab to the good folks at CME headquarters in Chicago. CME's recent actions certainly make it appear that the group's discomfiture with President Obama's suggestion to put regulators in charge of margin requirements "doth cause them to protest too much."

$33/Barrel Oil Now and Forever—With Leadership!

Posted: 06/03/2012, 11:19 AM EDT

One month after President Obama was sworn into office, the price of crude oil for West Texas Intermediate (WTI) was $33/barrel. Many thought it an anomaly, but it was a much truer reflection of the real price of oil on a genuine supply-and-demand criteria than oil's price today.

These last few weeks we have witnessed the beginnings of the rout of the oil speculators, together with their comrade-in-arms, the Organization of Petroleum Exporting Countries, better known as OPEC, which has forever been pushing up[97] the price of oil (and in turn that of gasoline) on the commodity exchange casinos, such as the New York Mercantile Exchange (NYMEX) and the Atlanta-based Intercontinental Exchange (ICE). Prices have eroded some 24 percent over the past few weeks to $84/barrel on Friday (but still some $50 over the $33/barrel price in February 2009), and that should only be the beginning.

Consider the following: new drilling techniques have located vast new reservoirs of what is designated as "shale natural gas," making us fully gas independent. (Up to just a few years ago, we were importing natural gas as LNG [liquefied natural gas] at terminals along the Eastern Seaboard at much, much higher prices per MMBtu). Natural gas is priced today at less than $2.50/MMBtu. At that price, the energy deliverable at $2.50/MMBtu would require WTI crude oil to be priced at $15/barrel in order to be competitive—less than half the price of $33/barrel at the outset of the Obama administration—thereby raising the emerging prospect of CNG (compressed natural gas) as a transportation fuel replacing gasoline, first in trucks and then in a growing fleet of flex-fuel cars, in a not very distant future.

And yet, largely unbeknownst to the public, and certainly barely heralded by the press or our deeply somnolent Department of Energy (DOE), is the realization that our riches in "shale oil" surpass by far those of our newfound bounty of "shale gas". Even without a federal government program of support, our shale oil deposits are already being accessed through the oil industry's initiative in such locales as North Dakota, with its rapidly growing oil production and its resulting and startling economic boom.

Some three weeks ago, on May 10, the director of natural resources and environment for the Government Accountability Office (GAO), Anu K. Mittal, delivered some staggeringly, eye-opening testimony to the House Science Subcommittee on Energy and Environment.[98] As reported by CNSnews.com's Terence P. Jeffrey, here is what Mittal had to say:

> The USGS [US Geological Survey] estimates that the Green River Formation contains about 3 trillion barrels of oil. And about half of this may be recoverable, depending on available technology and economic conditions. The Rand Corporation, a nonprofit research organization, estimates 30 to 60 percent of the oil shale in the Green River Formation can be recovered. At the midpoint of this estimate almost half of the 3 trillion barrels would be recoverable. This is an amount about equal to the entire world's proven oil reserves.

In her oral statement before the subcommittee Mittal pointed out what should have been immediately apparent to the administration, the press, and the financial community: that developing "the shale oil would create wealth and jobs for the country."

The testimony also bore out that most of the Green River shale oil deposits were on federal land. That said and understood, can anyone think of a more formidable national undertaking than the creation of a Green River Authority? This would be akin to the brilliant New Deal program, the Tennessee Valley Authority (TVA), a national undertaking initiated by President Franklin Delano Roosevelt during the Great Depression in order to harness the river energy of an entire region of the country, and, in turn, playing a key role in bringing much of the Southern economy out of the depths of that depression. As our economic crisis continues to deepen, what better initiative than a program that would not only make the entire nation energy independent but also allow it to regain its place as an energy leader. The resulting lower energy prices would be a core stimulant to an economy in dire need of help. Yes, there are and will be issues of environmental impact, but the experience of North Dakota and the successful development of shale natural gas throughout much of the nation shows that it can be done.

President Obama, President Roosevelt is beckoning.

OPEC Meets This Week, Holding the World Hostage to Its Budget "Needs"

Posted: 06/11/2012, 7:16 AM EDT

Ah, the Arab Spring! How convenient for it to alight just when oil prices were once again going through the roof. Saudi Arabia and its OPEC brethren are trying so hard to make us understand that their need for higher oil prices is now more essential than ever before. They cite the sharp increase in budgetary spending required in response to the Arab Spring, to keep their restive populations in check.

In other words, folks, the message is this: You like the Arab Spring? Well, then, pay for it through higher oil prices. This is akin to France proclaiming, "We need you to make up for our budget shortfall, so we will significantly increase the price of Camembert fromage exports." Yes, yes, I realize our passion for Camembert doesn't compare to our need for crude oil and petroleum products, but you get the idea; the concept is about the same.

The irony is that we (the United States and oil consumers throughout the world) are being asked to bail out the budgets of OPEC nations, especially the booming Gulf Arab States (Saudi Arabia, Kuwait, UAE, et al.), while we, and much of the rest of the world, are sinking into recession, if not depression. Saudi Arabia seems poised to rein in production to protect a price of $100/barrel for Brent crude. To support its objectives, earlier this month it raised[99] the price of its main crude grade, Arab Light, to Asian customers, according to the Centre of Global Energy Studies in London. Wittingly or unwittingly, this is making Iranian oil that much more attractive to these very same buyers—and, of course, in case you missed the point, it's a clear signal from the Saudis that the price for Brent crude better not sink below $100/barrel.

Given the prosperity of the Gulf Arab States, who are nonetheless piggybacking on extortionist oil prices while the world's economies are reeling, it is well past time for those in charge of our government, to take a stand. This is especially true now, given our growing domestic production of oil and gas, which brings us to the cusp of energy independence, freedom from all dependence on Persian Gulf and Eastern Hemisphere oil supplies and natural gas supplies altogether. Yes, it's time for our leaders to take the initiative to whisper sweet somethings into OPEC's assembled ears before that cartel's upcoming meeting, somewhat along the following lines:

> Gentlemen, your oil cartel game in restraint of free trade in oil markets has gone on for too long. It's time you bellied up to the bar and paid your fair share to rectify one the greatest economic distortions, shell games, and hijackings in human experience. If you continue to obstruct a free market in oil pricing, we the United States will in short order withdraw our naval task force plying the Persian Gulf at a cost to America's citizens of hundreds of millions a day, and leave you and your coastline undefended by us. We would, of course, wish you well in dealing on your own with your neighbor Iran and its murderously bellicose ambitions. And, of course, we wish you good luck!

The Jamie Dimon "Puppet Show"

Posted: 06/14/2012, 11:04 AM EDT

As but one example of a widespread reaction, "too cozy" and "ridiculous" were among the adjectives applied to the testimony of Jamie Dimon, chairman and CEO of JPMorgan Chase, given during the hearing before the Senate Committee on Banking, Housing, and Urban Affairs. This hearing appeared on CNN last night (*John King Show*), evidence of the extensive frustration felt by those who wanted hard answers to hard questions. [Please also see "C-SPAN Oversight Hearing on JPMorgan Chase," http://www.c-spanvideo.org/program/305501-1.]

What we did get was a wonderful performance in contrition—you know, losing $2 billion is human, and that sort of thing. But remarkably, with little push back from the assembled solons, Dimon claimed, straight-faced, "I don't know what the Volcker rule is; it hasn't been written yet."[100] This from a man who may not know Mr. Volcker's rule, but knows enough about him to have been quoted as saying, "Paul Volcker, by his own admission, has said he doesn't understand capital markets. He has proven that to me."[101]

This from the head of a so-called bank, who seems at loss as to how to distinguish between proprietary trading and hedging, a "bank" that has spent into the billions under his (Dimon's) suzerainty, expanding their proprietary trading capabilities by acquiring[102] the prop-trading divisions of Bear Stearns and UBS, and thereafter the Royal Bank of Scotland (RBS)'s Sempra Commodities, becoming the largest investor[103] in the London Metal Exchange (LME), extensively poaching traders and executives from rivals, and boosting their trading workforce from 125 in 2006 to some 1,800 by 2010.

Ironically, the day before the Senate hearing the "bank" announced[104] that it had hired an ex-Goldman Sachs energy trader to "expand its customer flow business amid tightening regulation over proprietary trading." Interesting language from a "bank" known to charter[105] VLCC tankers (very large commodity carriers of some two hundred thousand DWT [dead weight tons] or more), fill them with millions of barrels crude oil (termed "financial transactions" or "repurchase transactions," but for all intents and purposes largely "prop trades"), and leave them at anchor at sea. This means oil taken off the market when it might have had a salutary impact on reducing extortionary oil prices, then keeping the tankers anchored at sea for months at a time, while the public pays for it all at the pump and in heating oil costs. In short, these are immense cargoes paid with funds at near-zero interest rates accessible to the "bank" at the Federal Reserve window, all the while remaining custodian of billions of dollars in deposits guaranteed by the government through the Federal Deposit Insurance Program (FDIC). Their new hire could have been the focus of some interesting questioning at the hearings, but alas!

Oil is not the only gambit in play at Mr. Dimon's "bank". According[106] to the *Daily Telegraph*, the "bank" was reputed to have speculated extensively in the copper market, purchasing over a billion dollars of the metal and pushing prices to their highest levels since the banking crisis in 2008. Being major players on the very commodity exchange where copper is traded, their investment in the LME must certainly have helped.

As to Mr. Dimon's assertion of "I don't know what the Volcker rule is," a suggestion: when trying to look it up, start with the word *casino.*

HAS THE DEPARTMENT OF ENERGY GONE COMPLETELY OFF THE RAILS?

Posted: 06/19/2012, 8:02 AM EDT

Under Secretary of Energy Steven Chu, the Department of Energy (DOE) has almost totally abdicated its responsibility to the day-to-day consumers of energy (gasoline, heating oil, diesel, and so on). From the inception of the Obama administration, the price of oil (and in turn gasoline, heating oil, etc.) has skyrocketed from $33/barrel (for West Texas Intermediate [WTI]) in February 2009 to well over $100/barrel a few weeks ago, with barely any comment about these real-time distortions from the DOE; nor has the department come forward with any policy initiative to forestall this dramatic rise.

On the contrary, the DOE is shackled with the mind-set and outlook of its secretary, Nobel Prize–winning physicist Dr. Steven Chu, who continues to live in the aerie of academia. Secretary Chu remains in his ivory tower, seemingly divorced from the hard day-to-day tussle of the oil marketplace and its pilfering manipulation through the restraints imposed by the OPEC cartel, the distortions brought about by speculation and manipulation on the commodity exchanges—all costing American consumers billions upon billions of dollars more than if the market were a true reflection of supply and demand.

The Chu-run DOE's commitment to meaningful vigilance of the oil market's excess can best be demonstrated by Secretary Chu's own words (quickly modified after they hit home, but core to DOE's inaction over the past few years): "OPEC is going to do what they're going to do based on their own interests. I quite frankly don't focus on what OPEC should do; I focus on what we should do."[107]

This is in stark contrast to previous secretaries of energy, such as Bill Richardson, who did not hesitate to pick up the phone to call the OPEC nabobs to comment on their ongoing machinations and how they impacted the United States and its economy, even though he was roundly chastised by Iran's OPEC governor, Hossein Kazempour Ardebili: "In the forty year history of OPEC there has never been the case of the secretary of energy calling OPEC in the middle of an OPEC meeting … we are very upset and disappointed at external pressure, we don't like it."[108]

Ardebili's words made it seem as though fixing quotas to manipulate prices had become a divine right. Words that the then secretary of energy, Bill Richardson, could share with pride after having made those calls.

Not so with Secretary Chu. Let's not forget Chu's fateful interview[109] with the *Wall Street Journal* in 2008: "Somehow we have to figure out how to boost the price of gasoline to the levels of Europe."

The since-retracted statement is still troubling evidence of his mind-set, raising the issue of how and why, given the direction of his thinking, was he ever named secretary of the DOE? It's a bit analogous to appointing an individual as secretary of labor after that person said, "I don't much give a damn about labor unions"—regardless of whether he or she retracted the statement afterward.

There was also Chu's regrettable reply[110] to Representative Alan Nunnelee (R-MS) during congressional hearings this February: "No, the overall goal is to decrease our dependency on oil, to build and strengthen our economy"; as if the here and now, with frozen homes in Maine and family budgets being ripped apart, was not a core issue of his department's mandate.

Even his battle to "decrease our dependency on oil" has been deeply flawed, as with the $500 million-plus guarantees his department misguidedly extended to the highly questionable Solyndra project, a tab that the nation would pick up at the taxpayers' expense. And while the Department of Energy (DOE) staff was busy considering the likes of the Solyndra project, Chu was busy moonlighting on issues of "profound" relevance to the oil patch and alternative energy, such as publishing highly dense papers[111] with titles like "Subnanometre Single-Molecule Localization Registration and Distance Measurements" in such learned journals as *Nature*. With these digressions, focusing on what the likes of OPEC does or doesn't do, or how Solyndra was meant to make do, could well have become too much of a distraction.

But now, and unless I am missing something, comes an announcement whose timing is of such egregious inappropriateness that it appears to be mind-boggling. As though living in some far-off island unencumbered by current events and political tensions, the DOE brazenly announced[112] just days ago, almost on the eve of the scheduled nuclear talks with Iran in Moscow, that it would help the ailing the United States Enrichment Corporation finish its development work at its facility in Portsmouth, Ohio. "Under the new agreement we will be able to move forward with critical research ... while ensuring strong protections for the American taxpayer," Secretary Chu said in his statement. Representative

Edward J. Markey (D-MA) immediately took Secretary Chu to task: "The real risk of this nuclear bailout is for taxpayers, who will be on the hook for questionable government handouts ..."

Ominously, sources have also pegged the rescue as "vital to maintaining nuclear weapons and national security,"[113] almost concurrent with the nuclear talks that now seem to be going nowhere, where the point of contention is the very issue highlighted by the DOE's program: that of nuclear weaponry.

The DOE's announcement, and especially its timing, now smacks of hubris or stupidity or both, as it may have weighed on the negotiations with Iran, reducing the chances for a peaceful outcome through the willingness of Iran to halt its own nuclear enrichment program. If that is the case, Mr. Chu has a great deal to answer for.

Alan Greenspan Tells
It Like It Isn't

Posted: 06/25/2012, 2:28 AM EDT

On October 23, 2008, Alan Greenspan gave testimony before Congress.[114] As reported by the *New York Times,* "a humbled Mr. Greenspan admitted that he had put too much faith in the self-correcting power of free markets." The testimony reported on came from someone who nearly ten years before, as Federal Reserve chairman of long standing, was one of the most forceful voices in Washington clamoring for the repeal of the Glass-Steagall Banking Act of 1933, the law that had clearly prohibited banking firms from gambling with their depositors' money held directly or in affiliated commercial banks. Yet, when all is said and done, it seemingly becomes impossible to teach old dogs new tricks; certainly that is so in this case.

This past week (June 21, 2012) talking with Tom Keene on Bloomberg TV, Greenspan sprang to the aid of the Wall Street Mafia, militating to emasculate the Dodd-Frank legislation by proclaiming loud and clear that there is no need to return to the Glass-Steagall Bank Act and all it would imply in restricting the proprietary trading of banks. "Glass-Steagall was never a useful vehicle," were Mr. Greenspan's words[115]. The issue of proprietary trading—that is, the risk-prone casino gambling in the nonbanking related positions of commodities (such as oil, oil products, grains, base metals, etc.) or uncovered financial derivatives (such as CDs)—was swept into a homogenous category by Greenspan, who averred that banks are structured to take risks. This, as though making loans to businesses, industry, municipalities, or homeowners, and financing trade through letters of credit, were of the same construct as the rote commodity and financial-instrument gambles undertaken by the likes of Goldman Sachs, Morgan Stanley, JPMorgan Chase, et al.

Citigroup, for one, well understood this distinction, showing their responsibility to the banking community, company shareholders, and the economy at large after the financial disaster of September 2008 by divesting itself of its commodity trading division, Philipp Brothers, which at the time was among the largest oil traders in the world. This is in sharp contrast to JPMorgan Chase, the biggest bank proponent of prop trading and the biggest adversary of the Volcker rule core to the Dodd-Frank legislation. JPMorgan Chase, expended billions to acquire the trading divisions of Bear Stearns and UBS in 2008 and then the trading division of the Royal Bank of Scotland (RBS), Sempra Commodities, in 2010, thus making extensive investments in the gaming tables by becoming the largest shareholder of the London Metal Exchange (LME).

As extensively reported, JPMorgan's ambitious venture into prop trading was to have a huge unhedged (gambling) position in financial instruments blow up to a trading loss initially reported as a $2 billion wipeout, but now understood to be nearing $6 billion. Perhaps this is manageable for JPMorgan Chase, but such an extraordinary digression from traditional banking methodology has become common place, by JPMorgan's example. And with the support of the likes of an Alan Greenspan springing to the aid of the Wall Street Brigade and proclaiming there is no need to return to the Glass-Steagall Bank Act—and, by extension, to Dodd-Frank and its Volcker rule—such actions place our entire financial system at risk.

As an aside, the recent congressional hearings on JPMorgan's recent trading losses might well have been far more enlightening if questions were also posed to Dimon about JPMorgan's proprietary trading in commodities, such as crude oil, copper, and the like; specifically, exactly what such trading has to do with banking.

Harvard's Amazing Study Questions Today's High Oil Prices

Posted: 06/27/2012, 12:20 PM EDT

In 2007, my post "Peak Oil Is Snake Oil"[116] received much derision from peak oil theorists. Yet this month, the Harvard Kennedy School's Belfer Center published an amazing paper[117] titled "Oil: The Next Revolution—The Unprecedented Upsurge of Oil Production Capacity and What It Means for the World," by Leonardo Maugeri, under the auspices of The Geopolitics of Energy Project. The paper is a must-read for all who have an interest, or a stake, in all matters energy and oil—and the issues attendant thereto.

The paper has many salient points, such as:

> Contrary to what most people believe, oil supply capacity is growing worldwide at such an unprecedented level that it might outpace consumption. This could lead to a glut of overproduction and a steep dip in oil prices.

> The net additional production capacity by 2020 could be 17.6 MBD, yielding a world oil production capacity of 110.6

MBD ... (currently 93 MBD or 107 percent of demand
[MBD stands for million barrels per day])

Production capacity growth will occur almost everywhere,
bringing about also a "de-conventionalization" of oil supplies.
During the next decades, this will produce an expanding
amount of what we define today as "unconventional oils"—
such as US shale/tight oils, Canadian tar sands, Venezuela's
extra-heavy oils, and Brazil's pre-salt oils."

According to the report, the most surprising factor of the global
picture, however, is the explosion of US oil output. Thanks to the
technological advances brought about by the combined use of
horizontal drilling and hydraulic fracturing, the United States is
now exploiting its huge and virtually untouched shale and tight
oil fields whose production, although still in its infancy, is already
skyrocketing in North Dakota and Texas. The US shale/tight oil
could be a paradigm-shifter for the oil world, because it could
alter its construct by allowing not only for the development of the
world's still-virgin shale/tight oil formations, but also recovering
more oil from conventional, established oilfields. [Please also see
"$33 Barrel Oil Now and Forever—With Leadership," *Huffington
Post* (blog), June 3, 2012,[118] and "Energy Independence, Our Oil
Shale Deposits, Making OPEC Obsolete," *Huffington Post* (blog),
October 13, 2006.[119]]

The oil market is already adequately supplied. Global oil spare
capacity (the difference between the world's oil production capacity
that can be reached within thirty days, and sustained for ninety
days, and the actual global production) is probably at about four
MBD, which seems capable of absorbing a major oil disruption
from a big oil producer, such as Iran. In fact, the mere dynamics of
supply, demand, and spare capacity cannot explain the high level
of oil prices today. The only thing that can explain the departure
of oil prices from economic fundamentals is a combination of

geopolitical and psychological factors, including the deep-rooted belief about oil that still persists: namely, that it is about to become a scarce commodity. (Perhaps speculative oil trading should have been added, as described in "Are Our Leaders Hearing ExxonMobil CEO Tillerson?".[120])

The shale/tight oil boom in the United States is not a temporary bubble, but the most important revolution in the oil sector in decades. It will probably trigger worldwide emulation over the next decades that might bear surprising results, given the fact that most shale/tight oil resources in the world are still unknown and untapped. What's more, the application of shale extraction technologies (horizontal drilling and hydraulic fracturing) key to the conventional oilfield could dramatically increase the world's oil production.

The commentary here is, of course, just my interpretation. The paper goes on in fulsome detail about the issues cited above, as well as many others pertinent to the subject, including points touching on environmental concerns. Read it to understand how the oil nabobs have brainwashed us all to the adherence of this gross fallacy, holding us to that "still deep-rooted belief that oil is about to become a scarce commodity."[121]

Oil Price Skyrockets 9.36 Percent in Friday's Trading. Supply and Demand, Eh??

Posted: 07/02/2012, 11:30 AM EDT

Friday saw one of the biggest one-day escalations in the price of oil on the trading exchanges. The usual crop of soothsayers attributed the increase to news that Europe had taken steps to assist its banks, to the overhyped—in a world overflowing with oil—specter of political disruptions in oil markets, etc. Reasons that are hardly enough to explain away such a radical one-day jump. Clearly, other factors were in play. Short covering, of course. But, then again, the shorts were forced into panic mode. But by whom? And why?

Just last week, the Commodity Futures Trading Commission (CFTC) imposed[122] a $453 million fine on Barclays Bank for manipulating the LIBOR interest rate, and the investigation is continuing[123]. LIBOR (London InterBank Offered Rate) is the interbank interest rate central to global financial markets, along with a $350 trillion market[124] for interest rate swaps and over $10 trillion market of corporate loans that impact everything from floating rate notes to home mortgages to car loans, touching virtually every corner of the world's economy—much like the way that the price of oil impacts the price of gasoline, heating oil, diesel, and so on.

If a bank can manipulate such a vast market, is it not conceivable that a national entity, whose economy is deeply tied to oil prices, might well attempt to bring about an analogous manipulation?

Just two weeks ago, Aleksei L. Kudrin, Russia's former minister of finance, responding to ex-KGB operative President Vladimir Putin's boastful comments about the Russian economy, warned[125] that Russia's national budget "could become too vulnerable to a downturn in oil prices." To balance this current year's more modest budget, which does not include President Putin's campaign promises of higher wages, better maternity leave benefits, greatly expanded military spending, and so on, Russia (together with Saudi Arabia, the world's leading oil producer) needs an oil price for its European exports of $117/barrel or higher, according to Mr. Kurdin. The former minister went on to say that the Kremlin should brace itself for an extended price slump to $60/barrel or lower.

Back in 2008, as the price of oil was approaching $100/barrel, a single trader buying one futures contract on the New York Mercantile Exchange (NYMEX) was able to push the price to the $100 level and nab the bragging rights that went with it. He and his then firm, ConAgra, were subsequently fined[126] $12 million for making a "non–bona fide trade."

If one trade of one contract can move the markets, would it not be possible that a major player hiding behind a market-moving event, such as positive news on the European debt crisis, would use it to hype the commodity exchange trading to its utmost, far beyond a normal commercial reaction? A move of 9.3 percent, or $7.27/barrel,[127] in the price of oil is so massive that it is beyond commercial reason. And with 85 million-plus barrels of oil consumed throughout the world each day, it is a cost of staggering proportion to the world's economies.

CFTC, now that you have bagged one biggie, how about another!

Aspen Ideas, Natural Gas, Armenia Unheralded

Posted: 07/09/2012, 7:58 AM EDT

The Aspen Ideas Festival brings together, as panelists/speakers, individuals of tested competence and talent. Such was the case last week, with a gathering of Ray LaHood, the secretary of the department of transportation (DOT); Lisa P. Jackson, the administrator of the Environmental Protection Agency (EPA); and panel moderator, the eloquent and erudite Vijay Vaitheeswaran, senior correspondent of the *Economist.* These three took on the topic of "What Will Fuel the Automobile of the Future?"

Of course they touched upon alternative transportation strategies, such as electric-powered cars, biofuels, hybrids, and CAFE (Corporate Average Fuel Economy) standards, all of which can add significantly to the search for solutions to overturn our gas guzzling and addiction to fossil fuels.

Yet, given the current advances, Secretary LaHood went directly to one of the core issues: the game-changing potential of compressed natural gas (CNG), with its attractive price and vast reserves within the borders of the United States. A munificent resource now accessible through new drilling techniques can bring the nation to the cusp of energy independence. A fossil fuel, yes, but as a transportation fuel, it emits some 25 percent less in the way of greenhouse gases than petroleum-based gasoline, and, now domestically sourced, it is cheaper by far. Natural gas at today's quoted price of $3.00/MMBtu delivers an energy quotient that would require crude oil to sell at $20/barrel or less, compared to today's price of $85/barrel. Therefore, in terms of the environment, national security, and economics, natural gas is a win-win-win.

Secretary LaHood shared with the audience a story about his recent visit to Carbondale, Colorado, where the entire bus transport system had been converted from gasoline-powered engines to buses fueled by CNG. This is just one among many preliminary steps in a policy shift that in time will have broad implications for metropolitan transportation throughout the United States. But, yet, as we will see, it is only a small beginning.

Lisa P. Jackson, the fiery and hands-on administrator of the EPA, had her say as well. Inevitably, the issue of fracking came up, given its important role in the production of the newly accessible shale gas resources across the nation.

Some confronted Jackson to comment on a recent *Wall Street Journal* editorial[128] ("A Fracking Rule Reprieve," June 1, 2012) hailing the temporary suspension of federal fracking regulations covering everything from disclosure of drilling chemicals to well integrity as "redundant" to the plethora of state regulations, going on to berate the EPA (as in, "has tried to dig up pollution stories"), and castigating the Department of the Interior and the EPA for bringing on, in the *Wall Street Journal's* view, obstructionist and burdensome regulation hampering the production of gas and the expansion of these new drilling methods.

Jackson was fierce in her defense of the EPA's actions and policies. Significantly, she stated clearly and unambiguously her understanding of the enormous importance of this new resource and the potential that shale gas represents to the nation, in terms of both economics and energy independence. But, simultaneously, she was clear that it is incumbent on federal agencies to set standards in keeping with the environmental well-being of the nation as a whole and in the interest of future generations. Yes, drill and frack, but it must be done responsibly to ensure water safety and air quality, and federal agencies, such as the Interior and the EPA, must serve as guardians of the nation's environmental well-being. It was quite a performance.

But here we are on the verge of a vast change in our energy destiny, and, given Secretary LaHood's vision, veering in the right direction. Yet we still remain without a true national commitment to wean ourselves from gasoline to natural gas as our foremost transportation fuel. The transformation of occasional municipalities to natural gas–fueled transport from gasoline-powered engines is but a hesitant beginning. Consider Armenia!

What, you ask? And why Armenia? Barely known to almost everyone, Armenia leads the world in natural gas use. Seventy-five percent of its automobile and truck fleet is propelled by CNG,[129] an amazing accomplishment for a country hardly in the forefront of public discourse.

Showing the way, Armenia serves as an example of what needs be done nationally: a full-bore program to set up a national distribution system (pumping stations) for CNG, as well as incentives to Detroit and consumers to change over to CNG-powered cars. During World War II, Detroit retooled itself in six months and became the Arsenal of Democracy. With our government pitching in, it can this day become the arsenal of our energy independence and our environmental protector (insofar as natural gas is significantly less-polluting than gasoline emissions).

Let's show Armenia that we can do it too!

Jamie Dimon's Malign Influence on the Culture of American Banking

---

Posted: 07/13/2012, 11:41 AM EDT

Sheila Bair has called for compensation clawback of Jamie Dimon's pay, following JPMorgan Chase's massive trading loss. [Please see "JPMorgan's Dimon Deserves Clawback," CNBC.com, July 11, 2012.[130]] Bair, former head of the Federal Deposit Insurance Corporation (FDIC), was, until her retirement in July 2011, perhaps the only individual in government whom we could rely upon to view the financial crisis from the vantage point of Main Street and the pocketbook of everyday Americans, and to not allow the sway and swagger and political money of Wall Street and its plutocrats to besot her, as most of our government officials are wont to do. [Please see "Sheila Bair's FDIC Was Hated by Wall Street—And That's High Praise Indeed," CBS *Money Watch*, July 15, 2011.[131]]

Dimon, prior to his bank's massive trading losses, had been Wall Street's biggest proponent of proprietary trading. The fact that JPMorgan had not been taken down and survived without government intercession during the 2008 financial debacle had only convinced Dimon and his directors of the profit potential of prop trading. It encouraged a policy of expending billions to acquire new trading platforms, as though the bank's unscathed results of 2008 gave it carte blanche in extending its gambling "investments," and it used the 2008 results as the major talking point in trying to denude any regulation to rein in governmental oversight of such flagrant casino undertakings. [Please see "The Jamie Dimon 'Puppet Show,'" *Huffington Post* (blog), June 14, 2012.[132]]

Yet virtually no one focused on the real outrage: Why was JPMorgan sitting at the gambling table to begin with? Just because the spin of the wheel came out well for them in 2008 didn't mean the assets of the bank, its access to massive and cheap funding at the Fed window, with a government bailout assured as being "too big to fail," and its depositors' money (guaranteed in large part by such government agencies as the FDIC) should have ever been placed at risk (viz. the recent history of the "London Whale," and what more to come?).

But it was exactly that, rationalizing playing at the roulette table, that has done so much to destroy the nation's trust in banking institutions. Jamie Dimon, by his words and deeds, through his public persona, and with the massive resources of his bank, has become the poster child of such excess. He has used his position and the resources of the bank to organize a frontal attack on regulation, with massive lobbying efforts to denude Dodd-Frank legislation and emasculate its Volcker rule provisions, doing near-irreparable harm to the banking community and helping to destroy the public's trust.

Prop trading (gambling with depositors' money), together with the housing debacle, has focused the anger of the American people on Wall Street. Dimon has made himself the standout of both these excesses, and has used his position and the resources of the bank to exacerbate both excesses, be it through his frontal attack on regulation (trying massively to curtail regulation of the banks) and/

or JPMorgan Chase's excessively aggressive foreclosure policies toward homeowners, which reached its apogee when the bank foreclosed on servicemen and -women during their deployment in the field of operations in Afghanistan and Iraq. [Please see "It's All about the Money: Jamie Dimon's Big Pay Hike and the Home Foreclosure of Our Servicemen," *Huffington Post* (blog), February 19, 2011.[133]]

To show real leadership, this is the moment for Jamie Dimon to take his cue from Bob Diamond, CEO of Barclays. [Please see "Diamond to Forgo Pounds 20 Million Bonus Amid LIBOR Scandal," *BBC News,* October 7, 2012.[134]] And last, where is the accountability of the JPMorgan Board of Directors, who permit Dimon and management to inculcate and allow such an aggressive proprietary trading culture at JPMorgan Chase, at the cost of billions?

Banks in Collusion with the Fed Shamelessly Spike Up Price of Oil/Gasoline

Posted: 07/18/2012, 1:59 AM EDT

Whether it be LIBOR, the "London Whale," MF Global, and so on, all of which have recently come to light, what has hardly ever been a focus of public discussion, much less opprobrium, is the nefarious role the banks have been playing in lubricating the massive distortion of oil prices. The banks' role in the high price of oil was clearly set forth in congressional testimony[135] given by Rex Tillerson, chairman and CEO of ExxonMobil, who testified that the price of oil should be no higher than $60 to $70/barrel—while prices of oil and gasoline nonetheless continue to reach outside all bounds of supply and demand. Tillerson's position received further substantiation by Bart Chilton, the one CFTC commissioner who truly has the public's interest at heart. Chilton issued a statement[136] earlier this year focusing on the damaging influence that unbridled speculation has on commodity prices including oil.

That the banks have been playing a major role in the distortion of oil prices has been a constant theme of this corner over the years. And yet the banks continue on their malevolent way, without any governmental intercession and without anyone holding them accountable.

On Monday, July 15, the *Financial Times* laid it out clearly in the "US Banks Step Up Oil Trade Role."[137]

A sweeping overview of the broad inroads that such banks as JPMorgan Chase, Morgan Stanley, and Goldman Sachs have on the oil trade, the article describes their actions as, "wading deeper into the business of supplying oil as they compete with oil merchants selling crude to refineries" and in many cases taking delivery of varied downstream products as petrol, diesel, lubricants, etc. Ironically, the banks' increasing role in oil supply comes as US regulators proceed with rules limiting the size of the banks' oil derivatives positions. Yet banks are able to deal with these prospective limitations by using physical oil cargoes to offset their quota of derivative positions.

It is here exactly where the malignity of banks as oil traders takes hold, and where the near cost-free and near limitless borrowing from the Federal Reserve (Fed) window available to these bank holding companies distorts the playing field to the benefit of the banks' bottom line, as well as that of the oil industry—and to the massive detriment of the consuming public.

The outrageous use of physical cargo as a Fed-financed instrument of speculation in the oil trade, and as a forceful determinant in the ever-increasing price of oil, is not new and not isolated. In a post in this corner going back to 2009, Morgan Stanley was cited for having chartered the supertanker *Argenta,* with DWT (dead weight ton) capacity of over two hundred thousand metric tons, loading some two million barrels of oil, and then holding it at anchor at sea for months at a time. [Please see "Your TARP Money Is Being Used to Prop Up the Price of Oil," *Huffington Post* (blog), January 23, 2009.[138]]

Subsequently, there was JPMorgan Chase's long-term charter of the VLCC (very large crude carrier) supertanker *Front Queen*—another vessel in excess of two hundred thousand DWT (dead weight tons)—which carried a cargo of more than two million barrels of heating oil and which JPMorgan held as a storage/market gamble off the coast of Malta for a period of nine months. How many homes in Maine and elsewhere could have been heated with those two million barrels of oil? How many home mortgages could have been renegotiated with the hundreds of millions of dollars tied up as heating oil sitting at anchor off the coast of Malta? How high did JPMorgan and Morgan Stanley push up the price of oil and heating oil by taking this product off the market and then speculating for it to increase in value? And, last but not least, what role did the Fed play in financing this outrage? [Please see "Is JPMorgan a Bank or a Government-Funded Casino?" *Huffington Post* (blog), June 9, 2009.[139]]

The examples listed above are just some of the ones that repeat the constant theme of bankers playing "oil casino," a game that has now gone on for years. And no one has even whistled "Dixie."

There was a time when banks played a positive and essential role in the oil market. They financed production, they helped finance inventory, they facilitated the international trade in oil by issuing letters of credit making it possible for producers, or consumers, to bridge the formidable obstacles of offshore or second-party credit worthiness, permitting trade to flow unhampered.

But for them to now assume the role of principals—that is, taking title and attempting to influence the market in the direction of their position holdings—is close to unconscionable, especially insofar as they are the guardians of customer deposits guaranteed in large measure by the Federal Deposit Insurance Corporation (FDIC), and also especially insofar as they have access to the Fed window, a facility hardly meant to be an enabler of their casino instincts and betting posture that derives its profits from the ever-increasing price of oil and downstream products at the consuming public's expense. And, of course, it all falls under that ultimate safety net of "too big to fail."

Ironically, the last paragraph of Monday's *Financial Times* article advises that JPMorgan Chase and Morgan Stanley are lobbying regulators to carve out *forward* commodity contracts from the Volcker rule, which bans proprietary trading. Morgan Stanley, in a letter, warned that restricting banks' ability to compete in commodities would force customers to turn to trading houses, energy merchant companies, oil companies with trading desks, and/or other types of traders. Really?! As if the banks themselves had not become the very essence of traders, but with the help of the Fed and myriad government programs that have stacked the game to their gross advantage, to their enormous profit, and to the public's colossal loss. And by the way, those other traders are in the game with their own money and at their own risk, not piggybacking on the Fed's munificence and FDIC-insured deposits. (Just as an aside, Jamie Dimon, chairman and CEO of JPMorgan Chase, sits on the board of the New York Federal Reserve Bank. No conflict of interest there, of course.)

Today, Ben Bernanke, chairman of the Fed, will be testifying before the House Committee on Financial Services. Would it not be timely if he were asked about the role the Fed plays in facilitating the bank holding companies to hold sway in the oil market? Don't hold your breath.

Megabanks' Fed-Financed Backdoor Evasion of Prop-Trading Restrictions

Posted: 07/24/2012, 8:19 AM EDT

Ah, the charade continues. Just last week, Reuters reported[140] that "Goldman Sachs Expands Physical Base Metals Team," hiring a prominent physical metals trader as the "US Bank continues to bolster its physical commodities trading business." Thereby assigning to the lexicon another example of the more it changes, the more it stays the same.

Well, you see according to Reuters:

- "Banks have built physical trading operations."

- "End to prop desks turned banks to physical trading."

So there you are, simple and straightforward. Dodd-Frank imposes Volcker rule limitations on proprietary trading of derivatives, such as futures contracts for oil, copper, grain, and so on, so the banks go one step deeper and make an end run to avert oversight. They forgo derivative instruments and trade in the physical product.

In a normal world it would all make sense, but in this world of Wall Street hegemony over our lives and economy it becomes another scheme to rip off Main Street and everyone's wallet. Further, adding insult to injury, it presumes we are all dolts and that our government and our oversight agencies are asleep at the switch—or worse.

You see, it presumes that the restrictions on the prop trading of banks are meant to address trading of derivative instruments only. That the trading of physical commodities is outside the purview of Dodd-Frank/Volcker—a totally ludicrous and ridiculous interpretation hatched up by the megabanks and their lobbyists to permit them to continue the profitable wave of proprietary trading in physical commodities at our expense.

How is that, you ask? Well, first of all, what business does a bank have gambling on the rise and fall of prices of physical commodities? Yes, banks have a role in helping to finance the trade in these commodities, similar to its role in helping to finance trade in all products. But to become principals in this extraordinarily risky business, while simultaneously being responsible for the safekeeping of their depositors' monies guaranteed by Main Street taxpayers through programs like the Federal Deposit Insurance Corporation (FDIC), strikes at the very heart of what the limitations on prop trading is meant to achieve—and what it means to be a bank.

Second, and even more egregious, is the near limitless access these banks have (in the billions upon billions) to near cost-free Federal Reserve (Fed) financing, permitting them to gamble away in physical proprietary trading, and impacting, to their own benefit, the price and markets of vital commodities, and/or spiking, again to their own benefit, the price of other commodities, including base metals like copper. [Please see specific examples of chartering supertankers with millions of barrels of oil being kept at sea for months at a time, "Banks in Collusion with the Fed Shamelessly

Spike Up Price of Oil/Gasoline," *Huffington Post* (blog), July 18, 2012[141]; please see specific examples of spiking the price of other commodities, including base metals, such as copper, "JPMorgan Chase Banks On Buying Into the Casino," *Huffington Post* (blog), November 25, 2011[142].]

The Fed must desist in funding the trading operations of these megabank holding companies so that they can no longer use the Fed window to play casino with commodities that are basic to our economic well-being, and Dodd-Frank needs to be overhauled to prohibit banks from all proprietary trading in commodities, whether through derivative instruments or physical products. Period!

THE GREAT DROUGHT: AGRICULTURE, A HARBINGER OF AMERICA'S FUTURE

Posted: 08/06/2012, 8:47 AM EDT

The bold headline on the front page of the *Financial Times* some two weeks ago, "US Drought Triggers World Food Crisis Alert,"[143] reported that "the worst US drought in more than fifty years pushes agricultural commodities prices to record highs." The situation has only become aggravated over the past two critical weeks.

Accentuating the growing emergency, the *Wall Street Journal* would later inform[144] us, on August 2, that "Drought Dries Up Cattle Market," explaining that, faced with seared grazing pastures, ranchers across the United States who can't afford to provide food and water to feed steers and heifers are rushing to sell them, while feedlots are holding back purchases because of the escalating price of feed corn.

Clearly, a disaster in the making. A disaster not only for food prices in the American market, but portending a food crisis worldwide. It is an act of nature that has unsheathed a fact of fundamental significance, but barely touched upon in either political or civil discourse: The United States—with its vast expanse of fertile plains reaching from sea to sea, with its efficient inland waterways transport system, with its competent and professional farming community—has become, as the world's largest grower and exporter of corn, largest exporter of wheat, and second-largest exporter of soybeans, the world's food basket. It is a realization that will vest the nation with future choices of vast import and profoundly touch upon its character.

As if to underline the dimensions of responsibility that will be vested in the United States in this world so rapidly flattening by means of technology, this world with a burgeoning population necessitating the doubling of food production by 2050, an event took place in Cambodia that may well set the parameters of future discourse on this vital issue.

Just last month, Cambodia announced that, together with Vietnam, Thailand, Laos, and Myanmar, it would push for the formation of a Milled Rice Exporting Association. Cambodia's minister of commerce, Cham Prasdih, was quoted as saying, "The five countries will be the world's food supplier—what we could call the food basket of the world." Prime Minister Hu Sen (also of Cambodia) chimed in,[145] "When we form the association, we would have enough power to negotiate with OPEC."

Well, clearly what is good enough for a helping of goose and rice should be good enough for a helping of gander and corn—or soybeans or wheat or meatballs. Inevitably, this is the direction in which we are veering as the world's population grows and a planetary food crisis food looms ahead. Not only will billions of dollars be at stake, but so will the very lives of millions of the planet's inhabitants.

How will the United States engage this responsibility? Will we join forces with other major grain producers, such as Australia,

Argentina, Brazil, Canada, and Ukraine to form a Grain Growers Export Association (let's call it the GGEA) and then pervert the market as OPEC has done with oil, whereby we would play the role that Saudi Arabia plays in OPEC, as the major and indispensable contributor to the cartel?

Will we permit the continuation of unbridled commodity speculation on our poorly supervised commodity exchanges, allowing traders/speculators/gamblers who are free to hype the pricing of foodstuffs to levels grossly out of reach of the everyday consumer, let alone the offshore markets that have become dependent on America's harvest bounty? Just days ago, the *Financial Times* reported[146] that "Trading Houses Bet Corn Price to Soar," stating that "traders and hedge funds are betting that corn prices will soar to record prices of $9 a bushel or more as the worst US drought in half a century decimates the global corn crop. … The number of call options that would give traders the right to buy corn at prices between $9 and $10 in December has risen nearly thirteenfold in the past month…"

Can we, in the future, permit the trading houses, the bank holding company trading desks, and the vast plurality of gambling profiteers playing the grain markets, who are neither farmers nor commercial consumers, to push prices ever higher to their own profit and benefit at the cost of consumers worldwide, thereby becoming the arbiters of those who have access to food and those who do not?

These are serious issues of economic resonance, morality, and national conduct with worldwide implications. Given the devastation that this year's drought has brought about, this is a wake-up call that needs be addressed.

FRANCE'S 75 PERCENT MILLIONAIRES' TAX AND AMERICA'S INSIDIOUSLY CRAFTED TWO-TIERED LAW ENFORCEMENT

Posted: 08/12/2012, 9:55 AM EDT

Socialist François Hollande, France's newly elected president, has vowed to impose a 75 percent tax on any income above €1 million, which is equivalent to $1.24 million. Clearly there is growing concern among the upper echelons of France's business class as Hollande presses forward his "manifesto of patriotism to 'pay extra tax to get the country back on its feet again.'" [Please see "Indigestion for 'les Riches,'" *New York Times*, August 8, 2012.[147]]

The political rationalization for Hollande's initiative is to provide political cover for the deep cuts that the government may need to make to France's extensive social and welfare programs.

Yet the motivating force can be ascribed to a far more destructive impulse imbued with the class animosity dating back to the French Revolution. Significantly, Hollande has been quoted as saying, "I don't like the rich."[148] Voilà!

And that goes to the root of Europe's visceral response to the growing backlash against the wealthy, be it to the French everyman's historically uncomfortable relationship to money and class distinctions, and on to the cultural pervasiveness of that heavily laden German word *neid*, freely translated as "envy."

This European attitude has always stood in sharp contrast to one of America's great strengths, which is key to the US culture of economic advancement and opportunity: that is, the celebration of the self-made man. Here a Steve Jobs or a Bill Gates is both honored and regaled as having achieved the American dream, a dream that can be shared and dreamt by all Americans for themselves and/or their children. All of which brings us to what really lies at the heart of the issue: the growing backlash against the wealthy in this country.

In these United States, government agencies, peopled too frequently with those who are beholden to—or revolving-door alumni of—the very industries they are meant to regulate, do their work braying about financial settlements they have achieved from a plethora of civil fraud actions. Left unsaid is that, given the massive wealth of the companies involved, these settlements appear to be little more than a slap on the wrist and borne by the shareholders.

The oversight agencies are seemingly unaware that their task is of a much higher order. Their mission is first and foremost to keep in place the intrinsic values of what has made America great. For the Department of Justice (DOJ), the Securities and Exchange Commission (SEC), the Commodity Futures Trading Commission (CFTC) to achieve a moneyed civil settlement, paid out of the pockets of a company's shareholders, does not make up for the universal outrage at company managements walking away, not only scot-free to loot again, but also with their perverse bonuses based in measure on fraudulent earnings intact, and without fear of clawback.

It is an issue that gnaws at the American sense of fair play. It has conveyed to Americans of all means and background that the playing field has become fundamentally corrupted; that playing field had not always been perfect, but it was good enough to be cherished and recognized as one of the key impulses to American greatness and achievement. It has conveyed that our system has descended into a maelstrom of crony capitalism that no longer speaks to the American dream, and that we can no longer count on to enhance America's destiny.

It is clear not only that the playing field has become fundamentally corrupted, but that it has become so to the advantage of the purveyors of crony capitalism. It is clear that this is not the America that gave us the pride in accomplishment of a Microsoft, a Google, an Apple, an Oracle, a Starbucks, an Estée Lauder, a DreamWorks—the list could go on for pages. It is clear that now, even the extraordinary achievement of a Facebook can be brought to heel through the greed of its "bankster"-organized IPO, costing investors billions of dollars in losses, to the benefit of those who were insiders. It is clear that it has become a system of special privilege and access. Those on the inside hold all the chips, while Main Street goes down the drain.

Ironically, or perhaps propitiously, on the very day the *New York Times* regaled us with the "Indigestion for 'les Riches,'"[149] it also published another article, "Corporate Fraud Cases Often Spare Individuals." The latter focused on the increasing rate of civil penalties with fewer criminal charges, raising the issue that while collections have supposedly been a boon to taxpayers, the trend has raised recurring questions about the paucity of indictments at companies getting the stiffest penalties. The article quoted Senator Jack Reed (D-RI), chairman of a subcommittee that oversees securities regulation, as saying, "A lot of people on the street, they're wondering how a company can commit serious violations of securities laws, and yet no individuals seem to be involved and no individual responsibility was assessed."[150].

If the rule of law is not applied equally, whereby a teenager harboring a pack of marijuana gets jail time while executives who cashed in millions peddling fraudulent financial instruments remain untrammeled, the very edifice of America begins to crumble.

America's Increased Reliance on Saudi Oil Manifests the Bankruptcy of Obama's Energy Policies

Posted: 08/20/2012, 6:03 AM EDT

So far this year America's dependence on Saudi oil has increased by 20 percent, according to a front-page article in the *New York Times* [please see "US Reliance On Saudi Oil Goes Back Up," *New York Times,* August 17, 2012].[151] After nearly four years in office, the fact that the United States is even more dependent on Middle East oil is shocking testimony to the failure of the Obama administration's energy policies.

We are presently importing some 1.45 million barrels of oil per day from the Saudis, and, with the current US price for crude at $96/barrel, transferring $138 million/day to a regime that treats its women as mere chattel and has transferred billions to Wahhabi madrassas and prayer halls to propagate their poisonous anti-Western fundamentalism. As but one example of this, the *Times of London* had this eye-opening headline on March 28, 2010: "Saudis Fund Balkan Muslims Spreading Hate of the West."[152] [Please see "If You See Something, Say Something—The Failed Times Square

Bombing and the Price of Oil," *Huffington Post* (blog), May 13, 2010.[153]]

Ironically, much of our dependence on Saudi oil could be eliminated by the completion of the Keystone XL pipeline, planned to run from Western Canada to the US Gulf. The president, seemingly responsive to strident environmentalist criticism to the sourcing of Athabasca tar sands oil, has withheld approval of the pipeline, in spite of the fact that Canada is proceeding with the extraction project and will direct the output to other markets on the Pacific Rim if the United States continues to demur. A clear example of how this administration has it priorities upside down. But there are many other examples of the comprehensive failure of policies relating to energy these near four years past:

> In February 2009, a month into the Obama presidency, the price of crude oil touched the mid \$30/barrel and gasoline was under \$2.00/gallon. Today, we are choking on prices of \$96/barrel for oil and nearly \$4.00/gallon for gasoline. This is a misguided performance that speaks for itself, especially in that it has become clear the United States could have been at the cusp of energy self-reliance.
>
> Nearly four years into this administration, we are still without a coherent policy to access our vast reservoirs of oil and gas offshore, on federal lands, and in Alaska.
>
> Instead, hundreds of millions, if not billions, of dollars have been spent on failed alternative energy projects, such as Solyndra, and tax holidays for alternative energy sources, such as windmills. Alternative energy needs be a focus, but not to the detriment of energy independence and rational energy pricing. Consider the enormous benefits that would have accrued to the economy and our national security had even a portion of the funds and focus expended on alternative energy been allocated to developing environmentally safe fracking techniques,

giving us unfettered access to our vast holdings of shale gas and shale (tight) oil.

Next, there was the problematic appointment of Steven Chu as secretary of the Department of Energy (DOE). A brilliant physicist and Nobel Prize winner, but hardly equipped to deal with the rough and tumble of the oil patch, Chu's leanings were made clear in his comments[154] to the *Wall Street Journal* in 2008: "Somehow we have to boost the price of gasoline to the levels in Europe." That would have meant around $8.00/gallon. [Please see "Energy Secretary Chu, and the Price You Are Paying for Gasoline," *Huffington Post* (blog), April 16, 2012.[155]] Middle America would have said a heartfelt thanks. Sadly, it is a mind-set that has permitted prices to increase nearly threefold during Chu's tenure, without challenge or push back.

In addition, there have been no far-seeing policies to harness the extraordinarily huge deposits of shale gas that could wean us off our dependency on oil by transforming our gasoline-powered transportation fleet to compressed natural gas (CNG). Where are the government incentives for consumers, manufacturers, and distributors alike to undertake this core transformation? With today's price for natural gas at $2.70/MMBtu, crude oil would have to be priced at $18/barrel to compete with natural gas to deliver the same component of energy, not to mention the significantly lower carbon footprint of natural gas. For those who question whether it can be done, know that in the distant land of Armenia, some 75 percent of its automobile and truck fleet is fueled by CNG.[156] [Please see "Aspen Ideas, Natural Gas, Armenia Unheralded," *Huffington Post* (blog), July 9, 2012.[157]]

In 2008, the *Washington Post* reported[158] "A Few Speculators Dominate Vast Market for Oil Trading." It was determined that 81 percent of the New York Mercantile Exchange

(NYMEX) contracts are held by financial firms speculating for their clients or their own accounts. [Please see "Time to Dismiss the CFTC Chairman and His Commissioners," *Huffington Post* (blog), December 27, 2010.[159]] Since the inception of the Obama administration, virtually nothing has been done to either mitigate or corral the wild trading of oil contracts on the exchanges. The Commodity Futures Trading Commission (CFTC) is forever holding hearings or asking for commentary from the field, an elegant way for doing nothing. All this precipitated the president's moment of awaking from his reverie on this issue back in April 2011, when the Department of Justice (DOJ) was given the mandate to form the Oil and Gas Fraud Working Group. But we have not heard a single peep from this group, even now, close to one and a half years after its formation. Pointedly and materially, the nefarious impact of oil futures trading on the price of oil was highlighted in congressional testimony[160] in May of last year,[161] by none other than Rex Tillerson, chairman and CEO of Exxon/Mobil, the world's largest publicly held oil company. [Please see "Are Our Leaders Hearing ExxonMobil CEO Tillerson?" *Huffington Post* (blog), May 17, 2011.] During his testimony, Tillerson stated categorically that speculation was adding $30 to $40 to the price of each barrel of oil. Coming from someone of his stature and authority in the field, one would have thought action would be forthcoming. We shouldn't have held our breath.

The price of oil quoted on the commodity exchanges has increased by about 25 percent, or some $20/barrel, over the past 8 weeks, costing US consumers alone nearly $500 million a day (average daily US consumption of 19.5 million barrels multiplied by $20), a price increase that has gone far beyond issues of supply and demand, and far beyond potential flare-ups with Iran. Yet we have over seven hundred million barrels of oil in our Strategic Petroleum Reserve (SPR), in which we made a massive investment and which is doing us little good other than having made oil more expensive while it was being filled and taken off the market. It is an asset for which we receive little or no benefit and for whose drawdown there is no coherent policy. There is no realization in this administration that a broadcast willingness to release some oil from the SPR to counter abnormal price movements, such as those which we have seen these past eight weeks—and not necessarily even very much oil—would send the speculators scrambling to the hills and bring a degree of rationality to the trading floors of the exchanges, instead of the one-way bets that invite ever more speculation.

Last, but by no means least, what is sorely missing is a hard negotiating stance with our oil providers, especially those in the Middle East. The American public is laying out literally hundreds of millions of dollars a day in order to keep a massive naval task force in the Persian Gulf and in the vicinity of the Strait of Hormuz. The task force keeps the shipping lanes open for the Gulf States of Kuwait, Qatar, Bahrain, the UAE, and, of course, Saudi Arabia—all charter members of OPEC—all so they can freely ship their cargoes of oil to a world clientele, from China to the United States. Our armada also keeps them safe from the rapacious ambitions of their Iranian neighbor. We pay while they play. Only we pay twice: the first time by means of the OPEC cartel's induced and manipulated price of oil, and the second time by means of the vast sums required to keep a large portion of our naval fleet standing bodyguard. Something is very off base in this equation, and it is long past time that our government deal with the issue in hand and arrive at a more equitable arrangement—or possibly decide to just let our fleet sail away.

QATAR: INVESTING THROUGHOUT THE WORLD WITH OIL/GAS WEALTH, AND VISION

Posted: 08/28/2012, 3:43 AM EDT

The full page article in the *Financial Times* was a about a financial behemoth derailing what many had thought was a done deal: namely, the attempted takeover of the huge London listed mining enterprise, Xstrata, by the world's largest commodities trader, Glencore.[162] The article went on to touch upon the vast investments of Qatar Holding, offshoot of Qatar's Sovereign Wealth Fund. It is breathtaking in its diversity and reach. [Please see "Qatar Holding Comes of Age as it Resists 'Glenstrata,'" *Financial Times*, August 24, 2012.]

Qatar is a nation whose infrastructure was focused on pearl hunting and fishing, whose economy was virtually destroyed by the introduction of Japanese cultured pearls in the 1920s and 1930s. Then, in the 1940s, came the discovery of its oil, along with its enormous transformation from having a struggling economy to achieving one of the highest GDPs in the world. Proved reserves of oil exceed fifteen billion barrels, while reserves of natural gas are near twenty-six trillion cubic meters, or about 14 percent of the world's gas reserves and recognized as the world's third largest. All this was before the advent of recent drilling advances enabling access to the vast reservoirs of shale gas throughout the world, which in itself is looming as a game changer.

The article lists many of the varied and wide financial investments of Qatar Holding. These include not only a stake in Xstrata but recent investment in Citic (one of China's largest investment firms backed by its immense sovereign wealth fund), large holdings in Volkswagen, Porsche, Banco Santander Brazil, Barclays, Credit Suisse, J. Sainsbury, Harrods, Canary Wharf, Agricultural Bank of China, LVMH, Tiffany and Company, as well stakes in Shell and Siemens, Miramax Films in the United States, and the Paris-St. Germain football club. This is but a sprinkling, and the list goes on.

What was not mentioned, though certainly known by many, is that Qatar, an archipelago nation off the Persian Gulf coast of Saudi Arabia, is a nation with a citizen population of but 300,000, drawing its workforce from an array of Arab nations, India, southeast Asian nations, and other countries, for a total population in 2011 of 1,870,041 souls (according to the World Bank). According to *Forbes* magazine, Qatar is the world's richest country,[163] with a per capita income of over $88,000 in 2010.

Nor does the article highlight a particularly interesting and unique segue in Qatar's investment strategy. With a clear understanding that big is not always better or more effective, Qatar has immersed itself deeply into the financial sinews of the Grand Duchy of Luxembourg, a nation of 500,000 citizens. This effort has the purported ambition of helping to make that tiny nation Western Europe's Islamic financial center. Last year, Qatar purchased the Luxembourg operations of the Belgian Dexia and KBC banks. (As an aside, Qatar Airways has also purchased 35 percent of CargoLux, Luxembourg's large airfreight carrier.) Qatar's strategic alliance with Luxembourg, a charter member of the European Union (EU), and then the fifth-largest steel producer in the world, has emerged as instrumental in the formation of the European Coal and Steel Community. The ECSC, the first international organization based on supranational principles,[164] became an organization key to helping Europe get back on its feet during the difficult postwar years and was a precursor to the EU itself. Since those years, Luxembourg has become an important and responsible financial center, eliciting the comment from the *Wall Street Journal* some years ago that ounce for ounce, Luxembourg is the most influential country in the world.

What will happen when two such ounce-for-ounce stalwarts as Luxembourg and Qatar combine their focus and energies is a tale yet to be told. But it's not going to be dull!

NOPEC (No Oil Producing and Exporting Cartels) Legislation: A Presidential Issue and a Test of Political Integrity

Posted: 09/10/2012, 5:06 AM EDT

This past weekend, the most auto traveled of the year, gasoline hit a record Labor Day high. It is well past time for all our branches of government, in the name of the nation's bludgeoned consumers, to stop playing doormat to the oil interests, most especially the machinations of the Organization of Petroleum Exporting Countries, better known as OPEC.

The United States is the world's largest consumer of oil, and instead of using its massive purchasing power to forge a level playing field in the oil market, it has consistently permitted OPEC, and oil interests piggybacking on OPEC's manipulations (to create ever higher oil/gasoline prices), to make us dance to their tune, hiding under the preposterous umbrella of sovereign immunity and permitting OPEC's collusive practices—all countenanced by an out-of-touch US judicial branch of government, as though sovereign economic aggression was analogous to not giving parking tickets to cars with diplomatic plates. This has now gone on for years, with a near fivefold increase in the price of oil since the turn of the century and with nary a push back from our government or its agencies.

Yet some years ago, in 2007, there was a genuine effort to change the equation in a fundamental way when Congress voted overwhelmingly, in defiance of the oil lobby and their allied interests, for the No Oil Producing Exporting Cartels (NOPEC) bill, so named because it would allow the international oil cartel, OPEC, and its national oil companies operating outside the law and hiding behind our sovereign immunity shield, to be sued and held accountable for what are clearly anticompetitive attempts to limit the world's supply of petroleum and the consequent impact on oil prices.

In defiance of oil interests, Congress voted overwhelmingly for the bill (70 votes to 23 in the Senate, and 345 to 72 in the House). This was an act of refreshing and courageous leadership by our Congress, only to be abandoned after President George W. Bush, that great stalwart of oil interests and friend of Saudi Arabia, made it clear that he would veto the bill should it land on his desk.

Anti-OPEC legislation has a long history, and varied forms of a NOPEC bill have been introduced some sixteen times since 1999, only to be vehemently resisted by the oil industry and its allied oil interests, such as the American Petroleum Institute and their legion of K Street lobbyists, all of whom are fully cognizant of the fact that the higher OPEC can push oil prices, the greater the profits for domestic oil companies. Then, of course, there is the diplomatic pressure mounted by potentially impacted national interests, such as the assertion of the UAE's oil minister, Mohamed bin Dhaen al-Hamli, when he made the not-so-subtle threat,[165] "If the United States wants to sue [OPEC] member countries, it's extremely dangerous."

In 2000, the failed bill took new form as the Oil Price Reduction Act and the International Energy Fair Pricing Act, seeking to force the president to reevaluate, or even suspend, economic and security ties to those states engaged in "oil price fixing to the detriment of the US economy."[166]

The legal loophole has not only permitted collusion among OPEC member states that are able to impact the price and availability of oil, but, in an equally insidious manner, it has also permitted their national oil companies, the instruments of OPEC manipulation, to control important swaths of America's refinery capacity, such as PDVSA, Venezuela's national oil company's ownership of CITGO, with its significant refineries in Corpus Christie, Texas, Lamont, Illinois, and Lake Charles, Louisiana, all of which supply 13,500 domestic gasoline stations and thereby have direct impact on US gasoline prices and availability. In addition to all this, on May 31, 2012, a valve-turning ceremony took place in Port Arthur, Texas, signaling the completion of the Motiva Enterprises refinery's 600,000-barrel-per-day expansion, making it the largest refinery in the United States. Meanwhile, Saudi Aramco owns 50 percent of this refinery, and Shell owns the other 50 percent.

Opportunistically situated in Port Arthur, with its access to the world's shipping lanes, this refinery is strategically placed to export petroleum-based commodities, such as gasoline, diesel, heating oil, etc., to world markets, taking pricing pressure off America's growing production of oil and keeping oil prices up, which is Saudi Aramco's primary strategic business, and Shell' is not far behind. Converting American oil to petroleum products can be viewed as an alternative method of exporting American oil, which in itself is prohibited by law. It is curious that the plant's 600,000-barrel-per-day capacity is almost the equivalent of America's new oil frontier, North Dakota, with its daily oil production of 600,000-plus barrels/day.

In the face of OPEC and oil interests riding roughshod over the nation's economic interests, the Obama administration showed its true colors in the eye-opening court case litigated during the past year: United States District Court for the Southern District of Texas (No. 06-3569) Spectrum Stores Inc., et al. Plaintiffs-Appellants v. CITGO Petroleum Corporation; Petroleos De Venezuela S.A., et.al.

The plaintiffs charged that the Venezuelan state oil company (PDVSA) is "liable under the Sherman Act for its participation in a global price-fixing conspiracy with the OPEC member nations and other private oil companies."

Given the issue of sovereign immunity, the court asked the Obama administration to file a brief commenting on the merits of the complaint. Incredibly, the administration filed an amicus brief upholding the defendants' argument that the plaintiffs had no standing because of the principle of sovereign immunity, and the Departments of the Treasury, State, Energy, and Justice joined the administration's filing. This was a sea change from not only the president's position, but also that of his secretary of state, Hillary Clinton, when both were serving in the Senate. Then senator Clinton was cosponsor of the S.879 (110th): No Oil Producing and Exporting Cartels (NOPEC) Act of 2007[167] sponsored by Senator Herbert Kohl (D-WI) on March 17, 2007: "a bill to amend the Sherman Act to make oil-producing and -exporting cartels illegal." As cited above, the bill was introduced in April of that year but was not enacted.

Then senator Obama voted yes for the NOPEC Act of 2007; meaning, in favor of making oil-producing and -exporting cartels illegal. Voting yes would have amended the Sherman Act, making it a violation for any state

- to limit oil production/distribution of oil/natural gas,

- to set or maintain the price of oil/natural gas, or

- to otherwise take any action in restraint of trade for oil/ natural gas

- when such collective action has a direct, substantial, and reasonably foreseeable effect on the market supply, price, or distribution of oil and natural gas in the United States.

On February 29, 2012, Senator Herb Kohl (D-WI), chairman of the Senate Judiciary Committee, once again introduced the No Oil Producing and Export Cartels (NOPEC) Act. Senator Kohl's clarion call is lucid and should finally be heeded: "Now is the time, with the people we represent seeing soaring energy prices eat into their family budgets, to finally pass this legislation into law and give our nation a long-needed tool to counteract this pernicious and anticonsumer conspiracy."[168]

Clearly, the bill has gone nowhere because it did not have the administration's support. And therein lies the crux of the issue.

Is the Obama administration as pathetically submissive to OPEC and oil industry pressures as the Bush administration was? How would they deal with this issue if they were given four more years? And not to be left out, how would a Romney administration handle this hot potato? These are important questions that need be asked now, before the election, so Americans will have an understanding as to whose side the next elected president is on: the oil barons or the battered American consumer.

Four Years after the Financial Implosion, Regulators Finally Begin to Ask Questions

Posted: 09/17/2012, 1:32 AM EDT

Finally, after four years of hesitation and stalling, US regulators have begun an investigation[169] of insider trading by those Wall Street executives who attended a private meeting with the then secretary of the treasury, Henry Paulson.

According to the *Wall Street Journal* article,[170] investigators are following up to determine whether Mr. Paulson suggested at the meeting that the government was willing to rescue the sinking mortgage-finance agencies Fannie Mae and Freddie Mac.

The SEC investigators are only now looking into whether the firms traded on information that Mr. Paulson may have shared. The issue of insider trading from information emanating from Mr. Paulson's office was a focus of ruminations[171] from this corner some four years ago.

First, there was the virtually open-ended access to Mr. Paulson by Bill Gross, head of Pimco, the world's largest bond fund, as chronicled in the eye-opening *New York Times* article[172] "For Hire:

Bailout Adviser," and the subsequent and extraordinary bailout of Fannie Mae and Freddie Mac and their subordinated debt. The *Wall Street Journal* labeled the event "Bailout for Billionaires," in a September 11, 2008 editorial.[173] As the editorial proclaimed, "Investing rarely gets better than this: buy paper you know carries a higher risk but also a higher return, and then have Uncle Sugar eliminate that risk so you can make a windfall profit." The result was a $1.7 billion payday, the then largest ever for Pimco. A post concurrent with these events, "The Bailout: The Bond Billionaires Piggybacking the American Taxpayer for Another Gilded Ride,"[174] ended with the admonition, "Wouldn't it be refreshing if someone in Congress asked a few hard questions?" To date, I do not believe anyone has.

In fact, hard questions, perhaps until now, have been few and far between, and rarely have they gone to the core of the matters at hand.

Perhaps the most egregious example is the single question not asked again and again: What was the nature of the conversations between Henry Paulson, then secretary of the treasury, and Lloyd Blankfein, chairman of Goldman Sachs? Between September 18 and 21, 2008, there were nineteen telephone contacts[175] between Blankfein and Paulson, as well as numerous telephone contacts between Blankfein and Timothy Geithner, then president of the New York Fed. The more-than-$180 billion that was pumped into AIG to keep it solvent included tens of billions to pay down exotic derivatives in full. Derivatives, before the government's rescue, were selling at less than forty cents on the dollar. Was the highly significant tidbit of information that was made public after the bailout by Timothy Geithner, namely that the Treasury found that the prospect of AIG's failure posed a grave risk to the economy, ever whispered[176] by Paulson or Geithner into Blankfein's ear?

Had Paulson or Geithner made that morsel of information available to Goldman Sachs at the time, it would have been worth tens of billions to Goldman, AIG's largest counterparty. Goldman's holdings, direct or indirect, of AIG credit-default obligations made up approximately 33 percent of the $62 billion counterparty trades on AIG's books. It would seem self-evident that with knowledge of the Treasury's preordained policy to salvage AIG, AIG's trading partners would have resisted any modification of their counterparty contracts to levels representing the then-discounted real-time value. At one point, discussions took place between the trading partners to write down AIG's obligations to some forty cents— but this effort did not meet with success, as Goldman refused to budge. Was this refusal based on information of the Treasury's willingness to rescue AIG, information garnered by Goldman during conversations with Paulson and Geithner? If so, it would have been the ultimate insider tip-off. Was it? I do not know. All anyone does know is that no one ever asked these questions.

The *Wall Street Journal* commented on Friday that the inquiry comes amid an "aggressive" government crackdown on insider trading. Really?! After four year of hibernation? Perhaps we are witnessing a new definition of the word *aggressive.*

Egypt's President Morsi Is Wrong; It's Not American Taxpayer Money That Has Purchased Arab Hatred

Posted: 09/23/2012, 4:39 PM EDT

Today's *New York Times* published an extensive summary of a ninety-minute interview with Mohamed Morsi[177] as a way of introducing Egypt's president to the American public.

The interview, of course, touched on many aspects of America's relationship with Egypt and the Arab world. Comprehensive and succinct, the interview portrays President Morsi as surprisingly candid and open-minded, displaying but one clear digression in either perception or honesty, when he said, "Successive American administrations essentially purchased with American taxpayer money the dislike, if not the hatred, of the peoples of the region, by backing dictatorial governments over popular opposition and supporting Israel over the Palestinians."

Well, perhaps those are the issues to be bridged in Morsi's view, but where he is decidedly wrong is in referring to "American taxpayer money." The money exacerbating hatred and misunderstanding does not emanate from the "American taxpayer" per se, but rather from the American consumer both directly and symbolically; that is, the American consumer of heating oil, diesel, gasoline, and so on. It is the hundreds of billions, if not trillions, that have been, and still are, transferred to Arab oil nations, funding their near limitless monetary support of Wahhabi mullahs and Wahhabi protocols. This funding most especially emanates from Saudi Arabia, as well as the rest of the Arabian peninsula, and it extends to Pakistan, Afghanistan, Indonesia, and most everywhere, enabling the preaching of jihad, the control of the curriculum of the madrassas, and the indoctrination of young minds with hatred not only for America, but all of Western culture.

Leon Uris hit the bull's-eye in his novel, *The Haj*:[178] "Before I was nine I learned the basic canon of Arab life. It was me against my brother, me and my brother against our father; my family against my cousins and the clan; the clan against the tribe; and the tribe against the world. And all of us against the infidels.'

The riots and demonstrations this past week throughout the Muslim world show how deeply imbedded these Wahhabi teachings reside, and how combustible they are. If there is true goodwill between the Egyptian and American interlocutors, these malign preachments should become the focus of real Egyptian-American dialog. It would go a very long way to establishing mutual cooperation and respect.

The Charade of the Iranian Oil Embargo

Posted: 10/02/2012, 9:28 AM EDT

The Iranian oil embargo is in force and has been somewhat effective, but not nearly as effective as it might be. The reason for this was spelled out clearly in the *Financial Times* headline, "Vitol Admits Iran Fuel Oil Cargo Deal."[179] Vitol is the world's largest oil trader, with an office in Houston and affiliates throughout the world. Conveniently, not its Houston office, but rather its Bahraini subsidiary, availed itself and the Vitol organization of the opportunity to buy the spot cargo of Iranian oil product from a non-Iranian counterparty and then resell it, presumably not at a loss.

The transaction raises the troubling question of how much Iranian oil and oil product cargoes are being traded outside the parameters of the embargo restrictions set in place to constrain the purchase and sale of Iranian oil. Oil traders like Vitol are an important part of the oil market, taking title to massive quantities of oil and its related products and redirecting them to consumers throughout the world. How are they monitored? How are they being used by Iran? Perhaps even more important, are they, as principals, availing themselves of the opportunity to eradicate the Iranian origin of the product they are selling, which, in effect, means that they are skirting the embargo?

The United States could, in heightened support of the oil embargo and in its own long-term interests, initiate a process that is long overdue. The United States should at long last recognize that, as the world's most important consumer of fossil fuels, our market is as important to oil producers as they are to us in supplying our needs. Even as our consumption diminishes, we will be the most important market for years to come.

That said, it should become a matter of national policy that we no longer allow oil producers to take for granted their access to our market, irrespective of their policies and/or pricing strategies, such as the OPEC cartel's price manipulation. Furthermore, our national policy should state that henceforward all imports of foreign crude oil/products into the United States should require an import license designating the country of production origin, not simply the port of shipment. Ideally, this would be a system put into place, with licenses freely available without the need to impose restrictions. However, given the example of not only Iran, but also such suppliers as Venezuela with its hawkish stance to push oil prices ever higher, combined with its confrontational, malign, and dangerously contentious policies, does it not make sense for us to have a program in place to limit or stop imports from those nations whose actions are inimical to our interests by simply refusing them or limiting oil import licenses? As our oil needs diminish when other supplies become available from shale, the North Slope, offshore, and, of course, alternative fuels, this will be even more in our best interest. Perhaps our ability to act accordingly would dissuade the likes of Venezuela and others from promulgating their hostile policies.

Clearly, one could argue that oil is a fungible commodity, whereby substitution or exchanges with other producers or traders in some measure could well neutralize the objectives of such a program. But all these exchange activities leave a trail, and if there is a willingness to institute a viable licensing program, this too can be dealt with effectively.

It is long past time for the United States uses its oil purchasing power as a strength, rather than an abject and character-distorting weakness.

Big Bird in Romney's Sights, and the National Endowment for the Arts Is Next

Posted: 10/07/2012, 12:22 PM EDT

Frighteningly, during last week's debate with President Obama, Mitt Romney directed his comments at the moderator Jim Lehrer, pontificating, "I'm sorry, Jim. I'm going to stop the subsidy to PBS. *I'm going to stop other things* [italics for emphasis mine]. ... I'm not going to keep on spending money on things to borrow from money from China to pay for it."[180]

Inevitably *and* frighteningly, the National Endowment for the Arts (NEA) will be on Romney's list of "stop other things." I say "inevitably" because Romney has already declared himself on this issue. In an op-ed piece penned by Romney for *USA Today*,[181] he categorically stated:

The Federal Government should stop doing things we don't need and can't afford. For example:

Enact deep reductions in the subsidies for the National Endowment of the Arts, the National Endowment for the

Humanities, the Corporation for Public Broadcasting, and the Legal Services Corporation."

[Please see "How I'll Tackle Spending, Debt," *USA Today,* November 3, 2011.]

As an aside, the budget of the NEA is $169 million, very small potatoes in terms of government largesse. Gratingly, this is $73 million *less* than the $242 million that Mr. Romney's Bain Capital earned in its takeover of the medical company Dade International, a company that was ultimately forced into bankruptcy. And that is but one example of his enormous profiting from relatively small investments in companies, and, ultimately, not to the benefit of the acquired. [Please see "After a Romney Deal, Profits and Then Layoffs," *New York Times*, November 12, 2011.[182]]

The suppression of the NEA, the NEH, and PBS would be a cultural and spiritual disaster for the nation. The arts, and our respect for and nurturing of the arts, are key to our lives as Americans. The arts help define our lives and are essential to an aspect of America that has always run deep and strong in our spirit: our willingness to go beyond the rote and routine, to define new dimensions in ourselves, giving us new vistas of entrepreneurship and the confidence to accept risk because we have been tutored in creativity and its wonders.

Please understand I do not say this idly. During Ronald Reagan's presidency, I served on the National Council of the Arts as one of President Reagan's appointees. Governor Romney may call himself a Republican, but he is not a Republican of the iconic stature of President Reagan. President Reagan fully understood the importance of the arts in relation to the formation of the nation's character. He understood that the NEA and the NEH together comprised our government's badge of honor in support of the arts. He further understood that his administration would be judged in meaningful dimension by his support of the arts through his administration's support of the NEA and the NEH. From the outset of his presidency, he was personally engaged in supporting the NEA, and he appointed a close associate, Frank Hodsoll, as its chairman. Hodsoll performed brilliantly and had open access to the White House.

In simple economic terms, it is amazing that a financial engineer like Romney, with all his experience at Bain, fails to understand the leverage the arts have had on entire communities, and how they further the economic well-being of the nation. One need only consider the beneficial gentrification of entire neighborhoods, once close to the abyss, and entire towns and cities whose character have been transformed by the cluster of artists who have gathered to take up residence and to form communities of skilled artisans. Not to mention the millions of museum visitors and the hundreds of thousands of Americans in gainful employment in managing and operating these treasured institutions. The wonderful sprawl of art galleries, concert halls, public theaters, and so on. How diminished our lives would be without them.

No, Mr. Romney, we are not borrowing money from China to pay for this part of our lives, though we would happily learn from them and from other cultures, just as they do from ours. The arts are not an American enterprise to be outsourced to China, or India, or wherever, as so many viable companies have been by you and other financial engineers. The arts are part of our heritage, and their sustenance and support is an inherent responsibility to those elected to the bar of the nation's governance.

Obsequiousness to Power—The IMF's to OPEC

Posted: 10/10/2012, 7:40 AM EDT

In what must be one of the most flagrant abasements of principle and pandering to power, not to mention a crushing void of good sense, Christine Lagarde, managing director of the International Monetary Fund (IMF), spoke at the Gulf Cooperation Council (GCC) in Riyadh earlier this week. The audience was comprised of senior officials from Saudi Arabia, United Arab Emirates (UAE), Qatar, Kuwait, Bahrain, and Oman, the lead battalion of the malign oil price manipulator, the OPEC cartel.

Here is what Mme. Lagarde had to say: "It gives me an opportunity to *thank* [italics for emphasis mine] the GCC countries for their ... stabilizing role in the global economy because of the good management of oil prices, and oil reserves."[183]

The managing director of the IMF issued these paeans to a coven of producers who managed to help manipulate a price increase of some 20 percent since their last meeting this June alone, in spite of the difficult economic realities throughout the world—other than, of course, those of the Persian Gulf States. The issues of economic stress throughout the world were highlighted by dire

134

warnings emanating[184] from the very same IMF within days of Mme. Lagarde's rite of absolution in Riyadh.

Mme. Lagarde, in one fell swoop, legitimized the outrageous manipulation of the OPEC mafia that is stripping economies around the world of hundreds of billions of dollars. Some time ago, we were piously told by that OPEC don, Ali al-Naimi, who, speaking on behalf of his King Abdullah, instructed[185] us that $75/barrel was a fair price. Today the price for Brent crude is $114/barrel, a price that brings hosannas of praise from Mme. Lagarde and carte blanche for even higher prices. She then complimented her assembled audience for their "good management," with Saudi Arabia alone having produced 9.8 million barrels/day of oil last month; this with an installed production capacity that is now 12.5 million barrels/day, a difference that, in and of itself, exceeds Iranian daily oil exports in the best of times.

Perhaps we should take Mme. Lagarde's effusiveness to heart and learn from her standards. If one of the world's most prestigious international institutions can render such homage to brazen price conspirators, we should act accordingly. Congress should immediately move to restrict the export of corn, wheat, and soybeans (the United States is the largest world supplier of corn and wheat, and the second largest of soybeans), placing responsibility with a single export agency whose aim would be to enlist other major grain-exporting countries, such as Canada, Brazil, Argentina, Australia, Ukraine, and France, to collude in restricting production and exports, to force up prices to margins enjoyed by the OPEC producers. Russia, an important producer as well, needn't join, but, as with OPEC, it could become a member in spirit, given its vast oil riches.

And when the first formal meeting of GEPO (Grain Export Producers Organization) is organized, Mme. Lagarde should be invited to address the assembled member states to extend to them her and the IMF's blessing. Amen!

The *New York Times*'s Natural Gas Mania

Posted: 10/22/2012, 6:36 AM EDT

Once a bee gets into the *New York Times*'s bonnet, it has a tendency to make a lot of noise, and it won't fly away easily. For reasons unbeknownst to mere mortals, the *New York Times* has an obsession with its reportage on the natural gas industry, and that obsession slips to the edge of buffoonery. This Sunday's Business section carried a vast three-page exposé on the insinuated malfeasance of stripping profits from the likes of the great unwary, such as ExxonMobil, which bellied up to spend $41 billion to buy XTO, a giant natural gas company, when "prices were almost double what they are today." [Please see "After the Boom in Natural Gas," *New York Times, October 21, 2012*.[186]]

"We are losing our shirts today," said Rex Tillerson, Exxon/Mobil's CEO. "We are making no money. It's all in the red." This coming from the head of a company that has booked humongous profits selling us all, directly or indirectly, at vast margins, gasoline, diesel, heating oil, and, of course, crude oil. For the *New York Times*, it appears that selling natural gas at bargain prices is a cause for condemnation.

Most bizarrely, these profound revelations come but a little over a year since the *Times* regaled us with another series of exposés: "Insiders Sound Alarm Amid a Natural Gas Rush" (June 25, 2011)[187] and "Behind Veneer, Doubt on Future of Natural Gas" (June 26, 2011).[188] Both articles are replete with source documents "whose names and identifying information have been redacted to protect the confidentiality of sources, many of whom are not authorized to communicate with the *Times*." [Please also see "The New York Times Flays Natural Gas to the Cheers of the Oil Industry, OPEC and Coal Producers," *Huffington Post* (blog), June 28, 2011.[189]] The thrust of those *Times* articles insinuated that the potential of shale gas abundance was being vastly hyped, interjecting terminology, such as "Ponzi scheme" and "replay of Enron." The articles then go on to excoriate the United States Energy Information Administration's then optimistic assessments of the potential for shale gas reserves, by implying that their research relies on "outside consultants with ties to the industry."

Now, a little over a year from the *Times*'s revelations, we are informed that there is a superabundance of natural gas, so much so that innocents like Exxon/Mobil and T. Boone Pickens are suffering a discomfiting interlude of negative returns on their natural gas investments, after having benefited in the billions from their other fossil fuel plays.

Giving credit where credit is due, the article does give a passing mention that the price of natural gas has made it possible for gas-burning electric utilities to curb price rises for electricity, for chemical and plastic plants using gas as feedstock to site their operations in the United States. That Dow Chemical, a major gas consumer, "has assembled a list of 91 new manufacturing projects and representing $70 billion in potential investment and up to three million jobs" because of the abundance of cheaply priced natural gas in the United States.

Again, most bizarrely, a key thrust of the article goes on to flay the banks and investment bankers who encouraged this massive investment in shale gas plays and the profits they garnered in doing so, presuming, perhaps, they were working for the Salvation Army.

"Abacus and Other Soured Deals," as Now Seen by the *New York Times*

Posted: 11/04/2012, 8:33 AM EST

The editors of the *New York Times* Business section seem forever determined to whitewash and sanitize one of the core causes of the 2008 financial debacle and those who were central to the meltdown: questionable CDOs and their sellers.

Consider the November 1, 2012 article entitled "Reading the Fine Print in Abacus and Other Soured Deals," published in the *Times* some four years after the financial crisis.[190] Presented as the top story in the *Times* DealBook, and edited by their financial star reporter, CNBC host Andrew Ross Sorkin, this article lectures us that "A common refrain from the financial crisis is that poor disclosure was a contributor, if not the cause, of the financial crisis." In addition, it avers that "Buyers … were misled or not provided full information concerning their investments. The results were catastrophic when the mortgage market crashed."

Even a term as strong as *catastrophic* is insufficient to fully describe the magnitude of the losses incurred by those who entrusted their investment decisions to the good name, and heretofore, solid reputation of the so-called financial-instrument peddlers hawking the likes of Abacus, Timberwolf, Class V Funding III, and so on, incurring write-downs of $420 billion, or 65 percent of their face value, while those (CDO) instruments issued in 2007 alone were losing a staggering 84 percent of their face value. In addition, this allowed those who shorted the CDOs to make billions because of their informed foresight—whether it was Goldman Sachs and their John Paulson–inspired trash cans or others of their ilk who were able to pass off decidedly questionable financial products, hiding the pitfalls in the boilerplate of the CDOs and using their once impeccable standing and reputation, not to mention personal trust, to sell these instruments. Such individuals clearly knew that the buyers, both sophisticated and otherwise, would rely on the reputation and standing of the investment bank's portfolio manager's selection, and they used that to their advantage when selling the questionable instruments.

The instruments were extraordinarily complex, and the seller knew that much would be based on the reputation and diligence of the seller, rather than the buyers' navigation of the instruments' opaque boilerplates. In fact, the very authors of the articles seemed at a loss to fully grasp the intricacies of the instruments in play, having first identified the CDOs, at the core of the debacle as credit default obligations, only to later issue a correction in subsequent printings: "An earlier version of this article misstated the name of the financial products that were in part blamed for the financial crisis. They are collateralized debt obligations, not credit default obligations."[191]

If so the authors, then not who?

The *New York Times* Business section, other than Gretchen Morgenson and the erstwhile Business column contributor (now Op-Ed columnist) Joe Nocera, has had a long tradition of *explaining* to us all the virtues of the actions of such institutions as Goldman Sachs, portraying them as innocent purveyors of caveat emptor. [Please see "The *New York Times*'s Timely Whitewash of Goldman Sachs," *Huffington Post* (blog), June 18, 2010[192] and "The *New York Times* Sheds a Tear for Wall Street Paydays," *Huffington Post* (blog), April 8, 2012.[193]] Yet, only recently, the editorial page has struck a decidedly different note. An editorial on November 2, "The Junk Is Back in Junk Bonds,"[194] highlights the growing danger in the construct of those instruments' underlying assets, and the growing risk to those investing in them. This time at least the *New York Times* is taking the initiative to forewarn and not simply to provide an alibi.

The Appointment of Our Next Secretary of Energy

Posted: 11/17/2012, 5:03 AM EST

"In the forty year history of OPEC there has never been the case of the secretary of energy calling OPEC in the middle of an OPEC meeting. ... We are upset and disappointed at external pressure. We don't like it."[195] These are the words of Iran's OPEC governor, Hossein Kazempour Ardebili, as quoted in the *New York Times.*

To his everlasting credit, it was the actions of Bill Richardson, then secretary of the US Department of Energy, that elicited these comments from the OPEC cartel, in response to the calls he made in an attempt to remind OPEC of its responsibility to the world's economy and not simply to maximizing its extortionist pricing policies.

President Obama's secretary of energy, Steven Chu, stands in sharp contrast to Richardson. Setting forth his parameters early in his tenure, Chu stated, "OPEC is going to do what they're going to do based on their own interests. I quite frankly don't focus on what OPEC should do; I focus on we should do."[196]

This coming from a personage who, remarkably, before his appointment, was quoted by the *Wall Street Journal* in 2008 as saying, "Somehow we have to figure out how to boost the price of gasoline to the levels in Europe."[197] That, of course, would have meant gasoline at over $8.00/gallon.

The results were inevitable, with oil prices rising from approximately $33/barrel and gas prices under $2.00/gallon in the first thirty days of the Obama presidency, to oil prices surpassing $100/barrel and gasoline prices topping $4.00/gallon during this administration's four years of oversight.

With the departure of Steven Chu as secretary of energy, the new Obama administration has a golden opportunity, given the vast gas and oil reservoirs underneath American soil, and newly accessible by means of the exploitation of alternative and newly applied drilling technologies. It is an opportunity to reposition the Department of Energy (DOE) as a force for national energy independence, an economic force for national security, and as a monitor and sponsor of rational energy pricing, thereby husbanding a mighty engine of economic growth. As such, the DOE could serve as any and all of the following:

> A government agency that would work with those government agencies directly responsible (Departments of State and the Interior, as well as the EPA) to facilitate the authorization of the Keystone XL pipeline so that environmental concerns are properly assessed, but also taking into full account the economic and national security benefits that would accrue to the nation.

> An agency that would act as the citizens' watchdog to assure that the oversight agencies, such as the Commodity Futures Trading Commission (CFTC), the Department of Justice (DOJ), the Federal Trade Commission (FTC), and so on fulfill their obligations to the nation's citizenry,

curtailing the excessive speculation, if not manipulation, that has had such major impact on oil and gasoline prices. To act as a counterweight to the commodity exchanges and their omnipresent lobbyists who continue to provide the gaming table, along with their rampant coddling of speculators[198], profiting together with the speculators at the expense of American consumers fleeced at the pump.

A government agency that would be responsible for the Strategic Petroleum Reserve (SPR), setting new guidelines for accessing its seven-hundred-million-plus barrels of inventory, especially now that the nation's consumption of oil has declined significantly and oil production from such as the Bakken and Eagle Ford fields is increasing dramatically to the point, according to the International Energy Agency,[199] that the United States will become the world's largest oil producer by 2020. The quantities held in reserve are becoming progressively excessive, so that the question becomes, how should the SPR best be used to stabilize rational pricing to the economy's benefit?

A government agency that would break OPEC's death grip on oil markets, leading the fight for the passage of the of the oft-rebuffed and lobbied-to-oblivion NOPEC (No Oil Producing Exporting Cartels) statute that would have withdrawn the sovereign-rights exemption from OPEC national oil companies, permitting the DOJ to institute legal proceedings holding them accountable for their collusionary behavior and their cartel inspired market manipulation.

A government agency that would have the opportunity, given our newly accessible and enormous reserves of natural gas, to seize the initiative toward converting our transportation fleet to cleaner-burning natural gas. The department would focus on the current bottlenecks of compressed natural gas (CNG) distribution, while creating the basis of a national dialogue leading to the production of CNG-fueled vehicles, first trucks and then, eventually, passenger cars.

A government agency that would have the opportunity to create coherent alternative-energy initiatives that are not based on politics or cronyism—biofuels, solar energy, wind energy, tidal energy, and so on—but not at the expense of expanding the domestic production and usage of our world-beating resource, natural gas, and taking full benefit of its enormously advantageous pricing and comparably ecofriendly properties, in lieu of coal and petroleum-based gasoline.

The next secretary of energy appointment needs be someone who has experience in the oil world, including a sense of the players and the issues involved. This is a special moment, as the nation is at the cusp of an energy revolution (given its newly accessible resources) that could dramatically enhance the well-being and security of the nation. An old industry hand would be ideal, if we had confidence that he would not simply be a plant of the oil boys' network. Much work is at hand, and this is the time for social engineering to come to an end. Only the best should be asked to apply.

To repeat the apocryphal legend about President Harry S. Truman, who, after he had nominated General George Marshall to become his secretary of state, was admonished by one of his staff: "Mr. President, I must inform you that General Marshall has made it known that he feels intellectually superior to you, and that he, and not you, should be president."

Harry S. Truman, president of the United States, looked frowningly at his aide, and, without a hitch, said, "You know, young man, he's damn right!"

It would be great for all of us if President Obama took Harry Truman's example to heart.

HAMAS ALIGNED WITH ISRAEL

Posted: 11/23/2012, 7:06 AM EST

Some four weeks ago, on October 20, 2012 to be exact, the *New York Times* published an article[200] on page four, just under the fold, that appeared more as a curiosity than as hard news: "Hamas Finds Itself Aligned With Israel over Extremist Groups." Given the events over the past week, the *Times* reportage has taken on new meaning, and, hopefully, this is an augury of better things to come.

The article opens with the following revealing observation:

> Hamas, the Islamic group governing Gaza and once considered one of the most extreme Palestinian movements, itself is working to suppress the more radical Islamic military groups that have emerged here … putting Hamas in the unusual position of sharing an interest with Israel.

According to the *Times*, "Salafist groups [jihadist extremists] have been active for decades in Gaza, engaging in charitable activities and Islamic education, and dependent on donations from supporters from abroad, mainly in the Persian Gulf States." That is to say, oil money from the likes of Saudi Arabia and Qatar.

After the Gaza elections of 2006, militant jihadists not only had Israel in their sights but also attacked restaurants and women's hair salons in Gaza. After a bloody and direct confrontation with the governing Hamas authorities in 2009, the number of attacks on restaurants and entertainment sites in Gaza has decreased significantly.

One can hope that the events of these last days, incited most certainly in part by Gaza Salafists, and in spite of its bloodshed by both sides, augurs a growing awareness initiated by the Arab Spring and on the Arab street that is beginning to draw hard distinctions between the perception of their faith and the extremist dictates of the Salafists' fundamentally conservative doctrines extending to the glorification of jihad.

If so, perhaps this past week's denouement will be an evolution reflective for many on the Arab street of a liberation from the deeply ingrained, conservative, and too-often murderous jihadi mind-set. Perhaps it is a sign that a highly vital step is in progress, aligning the people of the Middle East with a mind-set more in sync with the modern world, ranging from Asia, emerging Africa, Europe, and the Americas, whereby faith becomes a builder rather than a destroyer.

The article quotes a Salafist leader as saying, "We are being chased down by Israel, Hamas, and Egypt."[201]

Perhaps that's not such a bad combination!

Our Next Secretary of the Treasury: A Woman or Jamie Dimon

Posted: 11/28/2012, 5:26 AM EST

Warren Buffett, that "Oracle of Omaha," who at the height of the financial crisis, having invested billions in Goldman bonds, instructed us through every microphone or camera he could find that we should understand that all those wonderful Abacus deals cobbled together by Goldman Sachs, costing their client-investors into the billions (financial packages that Senator Levin [D-MI] termed as "sh*t" during congressional hearings), was just business as usual. In short, in Mr. Buffett's perverse interpretation of caveat emptor, the responsibility for deceit lay with the buyer. To Mr. Buffett, issues of trust and accountability were secondary to this new world of finance. [Please see "Mr. Buffett's New York Times Op-Ed. Thank You. We Feel Better Now," *Huffington Post* (blog), November 17, 2010.[202]]

Mr. Buffett has now given us his latest pearl of wisdom. During an interview[203] with Charlie Rose on Monday night, he proffered Jamie Dimon, CEO of JPMorgan Chase, as his suggested successor to Timothy Geithner, secretary of the treasury. Given the way

Wall Street has run Washington, and certainly not to Mr. Buffett's cost, this would be a natural extension of the old boys' network solidifying business as usual during President Obama's second term, with the Treasury deeply entrenched to Wall Street. Selecting Jamie Dimon would be a gift to the powerful investment bank constituency already plying their trade in the all-too-comfortable niche of "too big to fail." These banks are ever quick to place at risk their depositors' money, while having easy access to cheap and virtually limitless borrowing at the Fed window, permitting them to engage in highly speculative proprietary trading while emasculating the Dodd-Frank legislation meant to rein in their excesses. These are policies that brought us to the brink of financial ruin. It would be a gruesome revisit to déjà vu all over again. [Please see "Jamie Dimon's Malign Influence on the Culture of American Banking" *Huffington Post* (blog), July 13, 2012.[204]]

Mr. Dimon's propensity for speculative and proprietary trading came into the spotlight by means of JPMorgan Chase buying up new trading platforms, such as acquiring the Royal Bank of Scotland (RBS)'s Sempra trading division, becoming the largest shareholder of the London Metal Exchange (LME), placing billion-dollar bets on copper and other metals, boosting their trading workforce from 125 in 2006 to some 1,800 in 2010, and chartering VLCCs (very large crude carriers)—tankers of two hundred thousand DWT (dead weight tons)—filling them with millions of barrels of crude oil or oil products like heating oil, and keeping them anchored at sea for months at a time in order to play the oil market. None of this even broaches the subject of the ongoing London Whale imbroglio ("financial transaction" to some; "speculation" to others).

Mr. Dimon's vision for speculative banking didn't end with aggressive proprietary trading. Under his suzerainty at JPMorgan Chase, the bank became ruthless foreclosure enforcers, to the point of being in breach of the law[205], whereby members of our military on active duty in Iraq and Afghanistan were dispossessed of their homes, in contravention of the Servicemembers Civil Relief Act, and also whereby 4,500 servicemen were overcharged on their mortgages and/or threatened with foreclosure. [Please see "It's All about the Money: Jamie Dimon's Big Pay Hike, and the Home Foreclosures of Our Servicemen," *Huffington Post* (blog), February 19, 2011.[206]]

Concurrent with Mr. Buffett's musings, there has been a plethora of commentary about the possible appointment of a woman as our next secretary of the treasury, including *Huffington Post*'s "With Geithner's Replacement the Treasury May Get a Woman's Touch," on November 25, 2012.[207]

The opening line of that piece was: "Washington—The best way to make sure the next secretary of the treasury is not overly beholden to Wall Street might be to hire a woman."

Among those mentioned as potential candidates were Janet Yellin, Lael Brainard, Laura D'Andrea Tyson, Sheila Bair, Sheryl Sandberg, Carmen Reinhart, and Christina Romer.

Certainly there is a crying need to divorce the Treasury from the financial industry's influence. Among all the potential candidates, both men and women, there is one person that stands out—who, incidentally, happens to be a woman, hardly a defining qualification, where competence and experience are paramount. That person is the one person in government who, together with the now senator-elect Elizabeth Warren, during President Obama's first term, stood steadfast with Main Street against the full power and might of Wall Street and the financial industry. She is the then chair of the Federal Deposit Insurance Corporation (FDIC), Sheila Bair.

We are barreling toward a destabilizing schism in our society, where one interest group, the finance world and its allies, are running the nation to their own economic benefit, oblivious of the pain endured by their fellow citizens on the Main Streets of our towns, and in the neighborhoods and tenements of our cities. Bair was the one person who fought tooth and nail against the clubhouse fraternity that had taken over the fiscal soul of the nation. [Please see "America Needs a President Who Will Confront the Financial Industry's Hegemony over Our Lives," *Huffington Post* (blog), July 14, 2011.[208]] She was unflinching in defending the interests of the nation's citizens. She was steadfast in holding that shareholders and debt holders should take losses ahead of taxpayers and depositors. She was a stalwart fighter for mortgage modifications that would have helped homeowners. "Our job is to protect bank customers, not banks,"[209] was her mantra.

"We probably don't agree on a lot of the fiscal issues, but on financial reform we do. Most importantly, I think she's the person who is going to be independent and do what is in the interest of the state of Massachusetts. And we need more independent thinkers like that in Washington, people who will be against special interest."[210]

That was Sheila Bair talking[211] earlier this month about Elizabeth Warren, Massachusetts' newly elected senator—words that could imposingly and purposefully be applied to Sheila Bair as well!

Syria, Iran, and the Specter of Sarin Gas

Posted: 12/07/2012, 10:29 PM EST

This is something I had hoped never to be writing about; not because it's secret, but, rather, because it is so gruesome I had purposely never brought it up, nor was I ever inclined to discuss the issue. It is one of those kernels of information best left unsaid and best left to the depths of the subconscious, because dealing with it is profoundly awful.

Years ago, while in the Navy, I served as the Assistant District Security Officer of the Third Naval District encompassing the area from New York through New England. In preparation for those duties, I was thoroughly schooled in the horrific dimensions of atomic, biological, and chemical warfare—a singularly unpleasant accumulation of knowledge.

Then, and, as I presume, now, other than atomic annihilation, the most effective and notorious weapon in any arsenal of destruction was the existence and capabilities of the nerve agent sarin. Far more dangerous than the mustard gas of bygone days, and other more recent gas weapons, sarin has the ability to kill ruthlessly, with virtually no prospect of defense and with barely viable and available antidotes. A mere drop of sarin nerve gas on the skin of any human is enough to break down that person's nervous system and cause inevitable death. It is a weapon to be feared and resisted at all cost.

That the Syrian government holds large stocks of sarin gas is unnerving in the extreme. The slaughter that would ensue in its release would be enormous. That the stocks were permitted to be amassed is already a grave failing of national policies. However, given the precarious and bloody confrontations that the Syrian people are already suffering as a result of that country's civil war, what has become gruesomely unacceptable is the willingness of the Iranian regime to encourage the Assad regime to resort to chemical warfare—that is to say sarin warfare. As sourced by the AP and reported in the *New York Post,* "O warns Syria":[212] "US intelligence has also intercepted a communication from Iran's infamous Quds Force urging Syria to use toxic sarin gas against rebels and civilian supporters in the city of Homs."

Any nation so openly militating for the use of sarin gas is beyond condemnation. They and their standards become a danger to the world itself. The world need take note and clearly understand whom they are dealing with!

The Hyped Distortion of Exchange-Traded Oil Prices, and the Price You Pay for Gasoline

Posted: 12/18/2012, 6:03 AM EST

The price we pay for gasoline is derived in large measure from the price of oil as quoted on the commodity exchanges. We are told that these prices are a reflection of an unencumbered and freely traded commodity reflecting a true universe of supply and demand. Really?

The US benchmark for crude as traded on the New York Mercantile Exchange (NYMEX) is West Texas Intermediate (WTI) crude deliverable in Cushing, Oklahoma. Its price has been hovering near $90/barrel these past weeks.

This is in spite of the fact that storage capacity in or near Cushing is filled to overflowing. Cushing is nearly awash in crude oil, and yet the quoted price on the NYMEX stubbornly stays in the $85–95/barrel range.

Earlier this month the *Financial Times* pointed out that "Yesterday there was a $10 differential of Midland WTI to Cushing WTI. That puts us at $75 a barrel, approximately." [Please see "Texas Crude Glut Sparks Oil Price Swings," *Financial Times*, December 3, 2012.[213]] Far be it for the American press to instruct us on the true formation of oil prices.

Seemingly, the pressure of supply and prices in various parts of this country has little or no impact on the traded and posted prices on the commodity exchanges. It is becoming ever clearer that the exchanges deal in financial instruments that have left all vestige of actual supply, not to mention demand.

The issue is only heightened and brought home by the dramatic differential between surging Canadian oil production originating in Alberta, where producers are selling their oil at bargain prices of less than $45/barrel for viscous heavy oil. A qualitative difference, yes, but hardly reflective of the massive divergence in price. [Please see "Canada's Oil Becomes Cheapest in World Amid Glut in Alberta," *Financial Times*, December 15, 2012.[214]]

It is well past time for our government to take a serious look at the massive discrepancies in the exchange-quoted price of oil, and the price of wet barrels traded in the field. The oil companies and those allied to them would of course resist any scrutiny—not to mention the enablers, the commodity exchanges themselves, especially if they can continue to help turning high NYMEX exchange-traded prices as a rationalization for disproportionately high and ever higher gasoline prices, in effect fleecing the pockets of all American consumers.

Back in April 2011, amidst great fanfare, the Obama administration announced the formation of the Oil and Gas Price Fraud Working Group. [Please see "Obama Administration Announces Formation of Oil/Gas Pricing Fraud Panel. Really?" *Huffington Post* (blog), April

27, 2011.[215]] Since then we have heard nothing, not a peep, from this august body. Now, with this administration's new mandate in hand, it is time for its work to begin. The panel has work to do, and now is the time to do it!

Yoko Ono, Matt Damon, and OPEC versus American Energy Independence

Posted: 12/27/2012, 11:14 AM EST

There she was[216], on the December 26 letters-to-the-editor page of the *New York Times*, militating against the extraction of America's vast resources of shale gas and oil through fracking technology. Yoko Ono's condemnation is absolute and without equivocation or codified substantiation: "But the evidence shows that there is no amount of regulation that can make fracking safe." All this after a full-page ad in the *New York Times* some weeks ago and a monster billboard[217] hovering over New York City's byways, with its thousands upon thousands of car passers-by, screaming, "Imagine There's No Fracking," a variation of her oft-intoned, "Imagine There's No War."

In essence, to prohibit fracking, as is Yoko Ono's wont, is tantamount to ripping out the nation's rail system and all that it would entail to the economy, to the management of carbon gas emissions, to the workforce, to the well-being of communities, all because of the risk of an occasional train wreck.

Yes, fracking has its problems, and they became clear very early on with low-budget excursions into the new realm of fracking, with little oversight and little knowledge of the full dimensions of fracking technology. But within the few years since then, fracking technology has been implemented to source shale gas, technology has improved significantly, oversight has become singularly sensitized to the downside risks, communities have heightened awareness, resulting in rules of the road that take into account the need for constant oversight and regulation. In addition, the industry itself is clearly aware of the issues at hand, while, for example, racing for ways to recycle the water used in hydraulic fracking. [Please see "Drillers Begin Reusing 'Frack Water,'" *Wall Street Journal*, November 19, 2012.[218]]

What has also became remarkably apparent is that we are dealing with an American resource that is in such abundant supply that it portends to become a major game changer for our economy, bringing thousands upon thousands of jobs into the field and to ancillary industries that are supplying the infrastructure hardware.

That natural gas alone, as a substitute for coal in energy plants throughout the nation, will have a major impact on the reduction of carbon gas emissions, far greater than anyone could have imagined before the application of fracking technology became a reality. Furthermore, it will be a bonanza to our balance of payments, reducing in significant measure our need to import fossil fuels.

Its resources are so extensive that it further holds out the hope and prospect of converting our transportation fleet, first trucks and then, eventually, automobiles too. [Please see "Aspen Ideas, Natural Gas, Armenia Unheralded", *Huffington Post* (blog), July 9, 2012.[219]] Converting cars from gasoline fuel to compressed natural gas (CNG) would vastly diminish our automobile society's massive carbon footprint.

The economies of our shale natural gas are such that its abundance and low cost serve as a core feedstock in chemical plants producing a vast range of products from plastics to fertilizers, and this has ushered in a flood of plant construction and siting projects by world-renowned chemical companies. These companies are taking advantage of this vast and available resource at gas prices significantly below those in Europe and Japan, bringing jobs and revitalizing languishing communities.

But not if Matt Damon and his bankroller[220], Image Media Abu Dhabi, can help it. (As a reminder, Abu Dhabi is a charter member of the OPEC cartel.)

Their forthcoming film, *Promised Land,* is meant to frighten Americans, and whomever else, to resist the development of shale gas in their communities. No mention here of the long-suffering communities of Pennsylvania who have celebrated an economic renaissance through the development and extraction of natural gas from the vast Marcellus Gas Formation.

Abu Dhabi will be applauding heartily if their and Damon's *Promised Land* film, due for distribution shortly, permits them and their OPEC brethren to continue to fleece the world with their cartel-manipulated price of oil and gas.

Yoko Ono and Matt Damon, as Americans of singular standing, what a significant service you could perform by making your fellow Americans fully cognizant of the full dimensions of this issue. It is a gift to be nurtured.

OPEC's Massive $1 Trillion Haul in 2012 While Sowing Jihad

Posted: 01/05/2013, 10:37 AM EST

With the price of oil hitting a year-long all-time high, averaging over $111/barrel for Brent crude (OPEC's benchmark), the Saudi-led OPEC oil cartel will glom more than a $1,000,000,000,000 (yes, that's *trillion*) in net oil revenue, a record windfall in 2012. All this is in spite of weak economic growth worldwide.

Back in January 2012, with barely a touch of irony or shame, Ali al-Naimi, the Saudi oil minister, pontificated, "If we are able as producers and consumers to average $100, I think the world economy would be in better shape."[221] This from the very same oracle who instructed us some two years before that "You must understand that the purpose of the $75 price is a much more noble cause."[222] [Please see "'Noble' OPEC Criticizes the International Energy Agency," *Huffington Post* (blog), January 19, 2011.[223]]

This torrent of money flowing into OPEC, especially into the Persian Gulf States, raises the question of how this massive windfall is put to use, other than by providing fresh capital for the world's largest sovereign wealth funds: those of Saudi Arabia, United Arab Emirates, and Kuwait.

A troubling and emblematic answer can currently be found in Zanzibar. Zanzibar?! Well, just two days before featuring OPEC's triumphal results in 2012, the *Financial Times* ran a depressing article on December 28, 2012, "Radical Islam Puts Zanzibar's Relaxed Way of Life in Jeopardy,"[224] reporting that Zanzibar, home to some one million people and with more than two thousand Muslim schools that draw on a long tradition of moderate and Sufi forms of Islam, is on the verge of an alarming shift.

Frighteningly, the article reports, "Increasingly, parents are sending their children to better-financed alternatives in a process that is beginning to parallel that taking place across a swath of sub-Saharan Africa, from Somalia to Mali, where the growing influence of more radical forms of Islam can be felt." Those needing instruction on how that plays out in nations like Mali need only read "Islamist Harsh Justice Is on Rise in North Mali,"[225] in the Africa section of the *New York Times*, on July 17, 2012.

In Zanzibar, such organizations as the Al-Noor charity, set up some four years ago with money emanating from Saudi Arabia and Dubai, has established a nationwide network of madrassas, and every year pays for students to study in Sudan, Abu Dhabi, and Saudi Arabia—where Wahhabi Islam is practiced. The article quotes a teacher from Zanzibar, one Indrissa Ahmad Khamis, as saying, "People who go to Saudi Arabia, when they come back, they want to change everything." Unsettling to say the least, given a telling observation in the article: "Al Qaeda and other terrorist organizations draw their thinking from Wahhabism."

The malign influence of oil money through the support and influence of Wahhabism extends far beyond Zanzibar and the sub-Sahara. It has engulfed the entire Middle East, from the extremists joining the Syrian uprising, to the very sinews of the destabilizing influences in Afghanistan and Pakistan, where many of the Taliban were educated in Saudi-financed madrassas that teach Wahhabism.

Its reach extends to Europe, where Bojan Pancevski in Skopje, Macedonia, for the *London Times* reported on March 28, 2010, "Saudis Fund Balkan Muslims Spreading Hate of the West":

"Saudi Arabia is pouring hundreds of millions of pounds into Islamic groups in the Balkans, some of which spread hatred of the West and recruit fighters for jihad in Afghanistan. ... Islamic fundamentalism threatens to destabilize the Balkans. ... Fundamentalist Saudi organizations are clashing with traditionally moderate local Muslim communities."[226]

All that said, a number of further questions remain:

First, given the enormous liquidity held in their sovereign wealth funds, is any portion of these vast holdings used to influence the traded price of crude oil/oil product futures, thereby forcing prices higher in the commodity exchanges, to the enormous benefit of OPEC? It's already evident that the commodity markets trading in "paper" oil future contracts can be manipulated. But one example of this occurs in the *New York Times* article, "BP Loses Trading-Floor Swagger in Energy Market,"[227] which cites BP's cowboy antics on the oil trading floor: "Its market wagers on crude oil, gasoline, or natural gas can use both physical supplies, as well as paper petroleum—in the form of futures contracts and other derivatives."

Second, what portion of these funds is used to influence government policy by subsidizing Beltway think tanks and public opinion? This includes manipulation by the likes of Abu Dhabi Media, financing such propaganda vehicles as the film *Promised Land*, which denigrates shale gas and depicts fracking in a negative light—bordering on hysteria, and not the laughing kind—in order to derail efforts to achieve energy independence. [Please see "Yoko Ono, Matt Damon, and OPEC versus American Energy Independence," *Huffington Post* (blog), December 27, 2012.[228]]

Third, what portion of their cartel-derived bounty is the Persian Gulf States prepared to reimburse US taxpayers who are currently tapped for some $100 million/day in order to keep a naval task force in the Persian Gulf to shield Saudi Arabia, et al., from Iranian aggression and to keep the sea-lanes through the Strait of Hormuz open, to the profit of the Saudis, et al., and at our expense? Our fleet is in leased facilities, in places such as Bahrain, docked in the metaphoric doghouse playing the role of watchdog, while the local pooh-bahs play in their mansions and yachts.

One last question: What is keeping the Obama administration and Congress from passing a No Oil Producing Exporting Cartels (NOPEC) law that would authorize the Department of Justice (DOJ) and the Federal Trade Commission (FTC) to take legal action against OPEC national oil companies? They have run roughshod over our antitrust laws, hiding behind tenuous and faulty judicial rulings that grant these companies sovereign immunity—especially Aramco, the Saudi national oil company, and PDVSA, the Venezuelan national oil company, both of which have significant refinery operations on American soil. [Please see "NOPEC (No Oil Producing and Exporting Cartels): A Presidential Issue and a Test of Political Integrity," Huffington Post (blog), September 10, 2012.[229]]

Will Chuck Hagel Be the Oil Producers' Plant in Our Government?

Posted: 01/31/2013, 11:18 AM EST

Chuck Hagel needs be asked many questions, but one overriding issue is Hagel's relationship to the interests of the oil producers from Saudi Arabia, Venezuela, and so on. These are questions regarding the formation of oil prices, and the interests generally of the oil and gas industry, whose history has proven all too often at variance with the American public's interests.

These questions arise because Hagel currently serves as a board member of one the oil industry's most aggressively international oil companies, Chevron Petroleum. Chevron has deep ties to Saudi Arabia and Kuwait, including its 50 percent interest in the highly productive partitioned zone, its five-year technology collaboration agreement with Saudi Aramco, its oil production in Venezuela, etc.

Chuck Hagel has been a board member of Chevron since 2010. On July 17, 2011, the *Wall Street Journal* article, "Chevron's E-mail 'Oops" Reveals Energy Giants Sway Over Markets,"[230] showed that

Chevron traders were holding oil and product contracts of twenty-seven million barrels in the physical and derivatives markets (an amount exceeding the total daily consumption of the United States by some eight million barrels), taking Chevron's trading far beyond the realm of hedging and into the realm of pure speculation with an insider's knowledge of the markets in play. And all this with the board's approval!

Board members of the large oil companies know the role that oil producers, such as Saudi Arabia, play in keeping oil prices high through the machinations of the OPEC cartel. In a sense, their own bread and butter is aligned with the pricing policies of such as Saudi Arabia/OPEC that can push the price of oil ever higher.

Consider the old adage "What's good for General Motors is good for the country." (Charles Erwin Wilson, Secretary of Defense, 1953–57.) Except that here we can say the reverse: what's good for Chevron and the other oil companies is bad for America. As a board member of Chevron, Hagel has played an important role in the fleecing of American pocketbooks. And now he is to be rewarded by being vested as our secretary of defense?

Watch out, America!

Secretary of Energy Chu Resigns, Leaving Oil Markets in Turmoil

---

Posted: 02/04/2013, 7:55 AM EST

In his letter of resignation from the post of secretary of energy, Dr. Chu characterizes his department as a "Department of science, a department of innovation, and a department of nuclear security." He then goes on to point out the myriad achievements and initiatives during his tenure, ranging from bioenergy research centers, to wind and solar energy initiatives, to nuclear safety, to appliance-efficiency standards, and on and on. It is not an unimpressive list of scientific and clean-energy programs. Embedded deeply in his letter is his conviction that rising temperatures present a present and growing danger to the planet and need be addressed. His tenure as secretary of energy addressed this issue relentlessly, and, even with the $500 million Solyndra debacle, built a foundation for research, creativity, and funding guarantees for a plethora of clean-energy projects supporting manufacturing plants throughout the country.

Were this his exclusive mandate, his four-year tenure might well be termed a success. But the Department of Energy (DOE) also has other fish to fry. The DOE's objectives relate not only to the environment but also, and quite profoundly, to the economy and to our national security. Energy—be it oil, natural gas, or coal—is a commodity key to the functioning of our economic viability, and here the DOE under Chu's leadership has approached disaster.

As an example, within a month of Chu's ascendency, the price of crude oil hovered around $35/barrel (and gasoline prices were well under $2.00/gallon). Today's price is over $95/barrel, even though our oil consumption is down some 2.4 percent from what it was four years ago, and production from the Bakken and Eagle Ford fields in North Dakota and Texas, respectively, has increased our domestic production dramatically, keeping our domestic oil market amply supplied (oil inventories are at or near all-time highs). In a situation such as this, it is the DOE's obligation to ask some hard questions, just as former secretary of energy, Bill Richardson, did during his tenure in the Clinton administration. Richardson, to his great credit, personally lobbied OPEC members, only to be chastised by Iran's OPEC governor, who said, "In the forty-year history of OPEC, there has never been the case of the secretary of energy calling OPEC in the middle of an OPEC meeting. ... We are upset and disappointed at external pressure."[231]

Richardson's actions stand in stark contrast to Chu's predilection, as witnessed by his intoning at the outset of his ascendancy, "OPEC is going to do what they're going to do based on their own interests. I quite frankly don't focus on what OPEC should do; I focus on what we should do."[232] And yet, he hasn't, and the price of oil four years into his oversight speaks volumes. He might not be the one to fully blame, but his Department of Energy (DOE) has done nothing to corral this vast increase in price. Rounding out the numbers in play, we consume some twenty million barrels of oil a day. A differential of $60/barrel ($95/barrel minus $35/barrel) results in a transfer of *$1.2 billion a day* from American consumers to oil interests here and around the world!

There are many other issues and tools that the next secretary of energy can address and enlist that have remained dormant under Chu, including the following:

> Engaging the Strategic Petroleum Reserve (SPR) and its seven hundred million–plus oil barrels in storage, bought and paid for by the American taxpayer, to counter economically crushing and irrational oil prices
>
> Propagandizing and shaming the Commodity Futures Trading Commission (CFTC) and the Federal Trade Commission (FTC) to initiate meaningful oversight of the distorted trading of oil contracts on the commodity exchanges (These are contract prices that, Rex Tillerson, the CEO of the nation's largest oil giant, ExxonMobil, has cited as being thirty to forty dollars higher than they should be, were not for the very trading of these oil futures contracts on the exchanges! My saying so is one thing; the CEO of ExxonMobil saying it is fundamentally another. [Please see "Are Our Leaders Hearing ExxonMobil CEO Rex Tillerson?" *Huffington Post* (blog), May 17, 2011.[233]])

Spearheading efforts to undertake organizing programs and policies to convert a major portion of our transportation fleet of cars and trucks to be powered by compressed natural gas (CNG) from gasoline in the years ahead. Given our vast newly accessed resources of natural gas, its attractive price and significantly lesser carbon footprint, this is especially crucial. [Please see "Aspen Ideas, Natural Gas, Armenia Unheralded," *Huffington Post* (blog), July 9, 2012.[234]]

The secretary of energy needs to understand that our economy, our national security, and the well-being of the American consumer are an important part of his or her mandate. These are the secretary's duties exclusively, of course, but without the active and hands-on engagement of the DOE, the "oilogopoly" has the field to itself, and the market discipline of supply and demand will fall by the wayside.

Putin's Russia Now World's Largest Gold Bullion Buyer—Why?

Posted: 02/12/2013, 7:48 AM EST

On February 10, Bloomberg reported[235] that "Putin Turns Black Gold into Bullion as Russia Out-Buys World," advising that the world's largest oil producer's central bank has added some 570 metric tons of gold over the last several years, for a total inventory of 958 tons. This while the likes of Switzerland, France, and the Netherlands were selling significant quantities of their gold holdings.

According to the article, there has been a long tradition of gold-buying/hoarding in Russian history, going back to the time of Tsar Alexander II, who ordered the government to start amassing gold bullion in 1867. Interestingly, the timing was almost concurrent with Russia's sale of Alaska to the United States for $7.3 million.

Yet purchases of gold under Putin have intensified to the point that Russia, as a matter of national policy and strategy, has surpassed all others in terms of the pace of its of gold accumulation. All of which then raises the question: why?

When Putin tells the central bank to buy, does he know something that the rest of us do not, or that we can only guess? Certainly, there is Putin's predilection, which he has made generally known, for viewing the United States as endangering the global economy by abusing the dollar. Or as the article quotes Putin's political ally, Evgeny Federov, as saying, "The more gold a country has, the more sovereignty it will have if there's a cataclysm with the dollar, the euro, the pound, or any other reserve currency."

All that certainly sounds reasonable enough, given the propensity of central banks throughout the world to print their way out of the current financially orchestrated economic morass.

But is there something else in play? Some two years ago, the Commodity Futures Trading Commission (CFTC) fined the commodities trading house ConAgra $12 million because one of its traders at the time, with but a single trade, purposely pushed the price of oil to $100/barrel for no other reason than to be the first to make this historic vanity trade:[236]

> CFTC Sanctions ConAgra Trade Group, Inc., $12 Million for Causing a Non–Bona Fide Price to Be Reported in the NYMEX Crude Oil Futures Contract
>
> US Commodity Futures Trading Commission release: PR5873-10, dated Aug. 16, 2010:
>
> US Commodity Futures Trading Commission (CFTC) today announced the filing and simultaneous settlement of charges against ConAgra Trade Group, Inc., for causing a non–bona fide price to be reported in the New York Mercantile Exchange, Inc., (NYMEX) crude oil futures contract on January 2, 2008.

The trader achieved this milestone by buying a single one-thousand-barrel contract on the commodities exchange, requiring a deposit of but $6,750, and thereby advancing the quoted price for oil by some $0.25/barrel to reach the first fabled $100/barrel print.

Consider this: if a single trader can move the price of oil, needing only some $6,750 as margin to do so, what can those trading on our pliable commodity exchanges achieve when using a war chest holding hundreds of millions, if not billions, of dollars?

On February 20, 2012, I wrote in this space, "Oil Embargoes, Sherlock Holmes, and the Russian Butler."[237] This piece touched on the importance of oil, and, manifestly, its price, to Russia's economy's deep dependence on the revenues derived from the sale of its oil and gas, positing the following:

We have a Russia governed by a coven comparable to our Wall Street ol' boys' network: namely, the alumni of Russia's highly touted secret service, the KGB. The KGB helped form Putin and many of his associates in government. Here was an organization that was the nonpareil master of clandestine intrigue, knowing how to keep secrets. Now in a sense, it is running the country, albeit with the trappings of democratic governance.

With the talent at hand, with its wealth, with the economic and strategic importance of oil revenues to Russia's well-being, and with all the stakes at hand, would it be a real surprise that Russia is doing whatever it can to keep the price of oil high and ever higher still?

Very probably, it is not the concern of the collapse of the dollar and other reserve currencies that is motivating Putin to gobble gold, but, rather, the core knowledge that the current price of oil is a manipulated mirage aided by his minions—a mirage that someday, whether sooner or later, will collapse upon itself. His motivator is likely that the trading at the commodity exchanges' oil-derivatives casinos, where the price of crude oil is currently pegged, is a rigged game. [Please also see "The Oil Market Plays Casino While the Obama Administration Acts as Croupier," *Huffington Post* (blog), September 10, 2011.[238]]. Now, while the going is good and the price of oil is high, is the moment to pile in the gold, as the mirage will eventually implode because it has no foundation in an unencumbered and freely traded marketplace.

THE KEYSTONE XL PIPELINE, TERRORISM, AND OUR NATIONAL SECURITY

Posted: 02/18/2013, 9:18 AM EST

Among the most-salient arguments in defense of the Keystone XL pipeline is the perception that the oil originating in Alberta, Canada, is from a safe and politically reliable source. This is in sharp contrast to current US imports of crude oil from the Venezuela of Chavez and the Saudi Arabia of Wahhabi indoctrination, as well as other suppliers from the OPEC cartel.

Canada, of course, is not an OPEC cartel member, and the policies of the United States have generally been positively aligned with those of its Canadian neighbor.

And yet something is astir that can only create concern, and that diminishes the rationale of the national security argumentation. It appears that the government of the province of Alberta, the source of the oil to be transported through the Keystone XL pipeline, has extended generous donations to Islamists with close connections to Hamas who are also promulgating the establishment of Sharia law. Organizations recipient of Alberta's largesse have in turn been linked to charities that had their status revoked by Ottawa for having funded terrorism. (The provincial governments of Canada have far greater sway than the states in our federal union.)

Alberta, north of our most-distant mountain states, is far enough away that we generally know little about its governance. Are these recent grants an augury of Alberta's future course? Perhaps the question that needs be asked now is: are we helping to fund a future danger on our northern border, and will the revenues generated by the Keystone XL pipeline help to create a condition deeply adversarial to our national security?

The Price of Gasoline and the Patently Absurd Application of Our Sovereign Immunity Law

Posted: 02/24/2013, 1:09 PM EST

The title of the article in Friday's *Wall Street Journal*—"Drivers Feel Pinch of Climbing Gas Prices"—says it all. Yet we have an anomaly in our courts, irresponsibly supported by the executive and legislative branches of our government: that is, the manner in which our courts interpret sovereign immunity, and, in turn, its impact on our day-to-day lives. Technically speaking, sovereign immunity is a legal doctrine by which a sovereign state cannot commit a legal wrong and is therefore immune from civil suit or legal prosecution. Yet here it has been extended by our courts, with the backing of our executive branch and the acquiescence of our legislative branch, to giving certain national commercial entities a free pass, allowing them to override our laws, such as those relating to antitrust and commercial collusion.

Quite incredibly, sovereign immunity has for years been extended to the machinations of OPEC cartel members and their very significant business interests in the United States. Just last May, a valve-turning ceremony took place at Port Arthur, Texas, bringing

175

onstream the expansion of the Motiva Refinery, now the largest refinery in the United States, owned and operated jointly by Saudi Aramco (Saudi Arabia's national oil company) and Shell (much in the manner of the Aramco-Shell SASREF refinery operating at the very heart of Saudi Arabia's petrochemical industry, Jubail Industrial City).

But OPEC's tentacles extend even further into US gasoline and petroleum product production and their markets. Here they have happily gouged American consumers through the OPEC-manipulated price of oil, the ubiquitous presence of Petroleos de Venezuela (PDVSA, Venezuela's nationally owned oil company), with refineries and facilities across the country refining and marketing gasoline, jet fuel, diesel, petrochemicals, lubricants, asphalt, and so on. These refineries and facilities are in Houston and Corpus Christie, Texas; Lamont, Illinois; Paulsboro, New Jersey; Lake Charles and Chalmette, Louisiana; Savannah, Georgia; and St. Croix in the Virgin Islands. All together, they have a capacity of more than a million barrels per day—all this while owning and running more than thirteen thousand gas stations throughout the United States and Puerto Rico.

Here we have Citgo and Motiva, two major players in the US gasoline market, both of which have parent companies with objectives that are not to produce competitively priced gasoline and petroleum products to service the US market and its pinched consumers, but, rather, to keep the price of oil high and have the quoted price of WTI (West Texas Intermediate, the US benchmark on the commodity exchanges) quoted at levels approaching those of Brent crude (the more international and significantly higher benchmark price quoted on the London Exchange).

Being tied to the OPEC cartel, their objectives can readily be alleged to be at clear variance with those of a stand-alone refinery needing to source its crude oil in the marketplace. The stand-alone refinery would do its utmost to procure the least-expensive source of crude and do all it could to reduce the price of oil in its procurement policies, thereby servicing the gasoline market at the most-competitive price possible. Not so with the OPEC Frankensteins! Given their cozy and open access to our markets, their objectives could reasonably be constructed to push up the price of the core input of the refining industry: crude oil.

Would the integrated US-based producers of crude oil and refined petroleum products, such as ExxonMobil, Chevron, etc., collude as to the output and pricing of their crude oil production, they would have long since been behind bars. A close look by the DOJ at the machinations of crude oil procurement of Motiva and Citgo could yield some significant and oil-market-moving/gasoline-pricing results.

Astonishingly, our government, most especially the executive branch, has been a staunch defender of the court's interpretation of sovereign immunity as it applies to the distortions inflicted on the American consumer by OPEC national oil companies. In the case of *Spectrum Stores Inc. v. Citgo Petroleum Corporation* (case no. 09-20084-C.A. 5. Feb. 8, 2011)[239], alleging that Citgo, as an oil-production company in its affiliation with the OPEC member PDVSA, was in violation of the Sherman Act and Clayton Antitrust Act, the court ruled for Citgo, citing the following rationale:

> Because the political question doctrine is jurisdictional, we address it first. When we do so, we discern that the complaints before us effectively challenge the structure of OPEC and its relation to the worldwide production of petroleum. Convinced that these matters deeply implicate concerns of foreign and defense policy, concerns that constitutionally belong in the executive and legislative departments, we conclude that we lack jurisdiction to adjudicate the claims. We hold alternatively that the complaints seek a remedy that is barred by the act of

state doctrine; that is, an order and judgment that would interfere with sovereign nations' control over their own natural resources. Accordingly, we affirm the judgment dismissing the complaints.

Astoundingly, in total disregard of the financial and economic damage that the OPEC-related oil companies are inflicting on both national and international economies, our executive branch has gone full-bore in siding with the court's decision by having the Departments of Justice, Commerce, Energy, and State all submit amicus briefs in support of the appellees (Citgo, et al.) and in affirmation of the judgment.

The legislative branch of our government has been more proactive on this issue, as described in a blog post from September 2012, cited below: [Please see "NOPEC (No Oil Producing and Exporting Cartels): A Presidential Issue and Test of Political Integrity," *Huffington Post* (blog), September 10, 2012.[240]]

> Yet some years ago, in 2007, there was a genuine effort to change the equation in a fundamental way when Congress voted overwhelmingly, in defiance of the oil lobby and their allied interests, for the No Oil Producing Exporting Cartels (NOPEC) bill, so named because it would allow the international oil cartel, OPEC, and its national oil companies operating outside the law and hiding behind our sovereign immunity shield, to be sued and held accountable for what are clearly anticompetitive attempts to limit the world's supply of petroleum and the consequent impact on oil prices.
>
> In defiance of oil interests, Congress voted overwhelmingly for the bill (70 votes to 23 in the Senate, and 345 to 72 in the House). This was an act of refreshing and courageous leadership by our Congress, only to be abandoned after President George W. Bush, that great stalwart of oil

interests and friend of Saudi Arabia, made it clear that he would veto the bill should it land on his desk.

Regrettably, the Obama administration has done little on this issue (as pointed out in the blog post above), other than to have its agencies file amicus briefs in support of our court's current interpretation of sovereign immunity, while American consumers struggle with gas prices that have risen by fifty cents in the past month alone.

It is incredible that at this time and under these circumstances we are giving a free pass to members of the OPEC coven, something we denied to John D. Rockefeller and his Standard Oil. At that time, the reining in of the Standard Oil monopoly was an act of national policy that was key to creating the freely competitive marketplace essential to America's emerging industrial ascendancy.

PRESIDENT OF THE MIDDLE CLASS

Posted: 03/02/2013, 9:31 AM EST

The "arbitrary and dumb" budget cuts[241] brought about by the sequester are indicative of egregious government mismanagement, most especially and quite precariously in these difficult economic times.

No matter the obdurate positions of Republicans and Democrats alike, the resulting indiscriminate across-the-board reduction in government spending, without giving any thought to national priorities, is an exercise in shameful government mismanagement.

That said, ultimately, we must temper the blame with the wisdom of Harry S. Truman's adage "The buck stops here."

The office of the presidency imparts responsibility and leadership, and no matter how difficult it is, the president's responsibility is to lead in the best interests of the nation as a whole. What we have witnessed is the abdication of that leadership by a president, who, given his myriad invocations and political focus, has turned himself from president of the United States to the president of the middle class.[242]

Certainly, the middle class has vast importance to the nation and is the bedrock of much of its economic cohesion. Yet its concerns, its needs, its nurturing—no matter how very significant—do not trump national priorities as a whole.

For President Obama to wrap himself in the mantle of middle class priorities is important and understandable, but not to the detriment of great swaths of the nation's interest, as has materialized by the across-the-board and indiscriminate sequester of government funding of national programs, from education to defense and on and on, as the president himself has pointed out.[243]

The president is meant to lead, and the responsibility of the collapse of the sequester negotiations rests squarely with him, no matter how difficult the issue. Harry Truman would have understood that clearly.

The JPMorgan Congressional Inquisition: "Déjà-Vu All Over Again"

Posted: 03/15/2013, 5:54 PM EDT

JPMorgan Chase has finally, finally been brought to account, as seen in yesterday's congressional hearings. The alacrity and seeming ease with which $6 billion were spirited away trading in proprietary derivatives by the London Whale, with seemingly conspiratorial oversight by top management, was breathtaking in its full-bore lack of assumed responsibility and mere hand-slap accountability by the perpetrators. Senators Levin and McCain could barely contain their disdain and outrage while suffering the self-serving and evasive responses to their incisive and deeply prepared questioning. In their demeanor and the tenor of their replies, the responders validated the earlier observations of Senator Levin, who called the bank's trading strategy a "runaway train that barreled through every risk warning."[244] (Senator Levin is the chair of the Senate's Permanent Subcommittee on Investigations.)

Yet this should not have been a new revelation, and it only speaks to how lax our oversight agencies are, given the excesses of proprietary derivative trading by institutions that hold government guaranteed deposits and access to the Fed discount window, but then, all too often bet the farm on prop trading instead of supporting the American economy with loans to businesses, builders, and tradesmen, as banks ought to do.

This space has focused on this very issue for the last five years, not only questioning its impact on the viability of the banks themselves, but on the pumped-up trading prices on such core commodities as oil and petroleum derivatives (from gasoline to heating oil), and foodstuff (from corn, to wheat, to soybeans, and on and on). These core commodities are essential to our daily lives. This issue is one of endless concern, with no real solution or accountability at hand.

The following is a list of past posts:

"Our Next Secretary of the Treasury: A Woman or Jamie Dimon" (November 18, 2012)[245]

"Banks in Collusion with the Fed Shamelessly Spike Up Price of Oil/Gasoline" (July 18, 2012)[246]

"Jamie Dimon's Malign Influence on the Culture of American Banking" (July 13, 2012)[247]

"The Wall Street Journal's Convoluted Whitewash of Jamie Dimon" (May 14, 2012)[248]

"The Volcker Rule and Wall Street's Pliant Media Plant" (February 15, 2012)[249]

"Alan Greenspan Tells It Like It Isn't" (June 25, 2011)[250]

"Bravo, JPMorgan! Just What We Need, Another Wall Street Casino" (October 12, 2010)[251]

"JPMorgan Shows Us the 'Volcker Rule' Is All Hat and No Cattle, While the Administration and Congress Fiddle Away" (February 16, 2010)[252]

"Did the Huffington Post Bring JPMorgan Chase to Heel?" (February 2, 2010)[253]

"JPMorgan Chase Throws Down the Gauntlet at President Obama" (January 26, 2010)[254]

"Our Banks Becoming Casinos, and Washington Yawns" (January 20, 2010)[255]

"Is JPMorgan a Bank or a Government-Funded Casino?" (June 9, 2009)[256]

"Wall Street Banks Blindsided Gambling with Monies Entrusted to Them" (January 16, 2009)[257]

JPMorgan Board's Abject Failure of Oversight

Posted: 03/23/2013, 3:08 PM EDT

In a classic example of crony board behavior, in spite of the grossly embarrassing Senate hearings highlighting massive fissures in JPMorgan's trading oversight and management, highlighting a corporate policy of proprietary trading, more clearly translated as rote gambling, that was not only countenanced but encouraged by management, resulting in the disastrous positions of the London Whale and its cost of billions to the institution, the board of directors of JPMorgan Chase announced on Friday that they would continue to support Mr. Jamie Dimon as *both* the bank's chairman and CEO. [Please see "JPMorgan Board Confirms Dual Role for Dimon," *New York Times*, March 22, 2013.[258]]

This is not only in the face of the huge failure, as detailed in the 301-page Senate report, but also in JPMorgan's intransigent dismissal of a wide gathering of shareholders demanding separation of the chairman and executive posts, including the American Federation of State, County and Municipal Employees, as well the pension funds of New York and Connecticut, which filed resolutions to separate the two executive posts.

And why not? Being on the board of JPMorgan Chase is a happy club-like sinecure, well compensated and without much risk of being held accountable. We can well presume that all the board members have the comfort of knowing they are the beneficiaries of the board of directors' liability insurance policy, which will hold them virtually harmless for any decisions, no matter how they might impact other shareholders. And, of course, the insurance would be bought, paid for, and expensed by the mother ship, JPMorgan Chase.

In doing so, the board is abetting a culture of risk taking that is placing our entire banking system in danger, all the while countenancing the indiscriminate and unregulated bank's gambling on such a wide array of traded derivatives, ranging from credit, to oil and petroleum products, to grain staples (such as wheat and corn), to base metals (such as copper and rare earths). The list goes on and on, while placing at risk depositor monies guaranteed by the Federal Deposit Insurance Corporation (FDIC), and while having access to near limitless funding at near zero interest from the Fed window—not to mention the banking system's impact on the upward and costly distortion of prices, ranging from gasoline to foodstuffs. (Please see "Jamie Dimon's Malign Influence On The Culture Of American Banking." *Huffington Post* (blog),)[259]

Oh yes, there was the slap on the wrist this past January, when, in the wake of the London Whale imbroglio, JPMorgan's board cut Mr. Dimon's compensation from $23.1 million to a mere $11.5 million. This was after the London Whale's hiccup of more than $6.2 billion (what we know of presently). Not a bad trade-off if you can get it, and Mr. Dimon still doesn't have to take the subway.

Oh, by the way, the decision to cut Mr. Dimon's salary came after a series of marathon meetings led by none other than Lee R. Raymond, the former CEO of ExxonMobil, who heads the board's compensation committee. In Mr. Raymond, Mr. Dimon and JPMorgan Chase have an expert in executive compensation to look after their interests. He knows how to get things done, having pocketed some $400 million as his good-bye handshake from ExxonMobil. [Please see "Exxon's Lee Raymond, 'Steward of the Free Market System,'" *Huffington Post* (blog), April 15, 2006.[260]]

When is Washington going to stop the talk and walk the walk?

Egypt's Looming Famine and America's Grain Bounty

Posted: 04/04/2013, 11:24 PM EDT

Headlined in the front-page lead column of the *New York Times* on Sunday, March 30, 2013, was this article: "Short of Money, Egypt Sees Crisis on Fuel and Food."[261] Going into the grim details of an Egypt at the precipice of an acute food shortage, including the desperate scarcity of wheat needed to feed a growingly restive population with subsidized bread, the article describes the situation as "stirring fears of an economic catastrophe." Negotiations with the World Bank and the IMF are foundering, given the tax increases and subsidy cuts demanded by these international institutions of an Egyptian government already struggling to quell the ever-mounting violent protests by its political rivals.

Egypt imports 75 percent of its wheat, making it the world's largest wheat importer. It is a commodity clearly essential to feeding its population. Egypt's current travails have decimated both tourism and investment, resulting in a grave economic downturn that in turn has resulted in Egypt no longer having the foreign exchange (hard currency reserves have fallen from more than $36 billion over two years ago to $13 billion today). Given this situation, to buy wheat in the open market without sellers involves assuming enormous credit risk.

Given the current construct of the wheat trade, that credit would have to be forthcoming from commodity trading houses, such as Glencore, Cargill/Tradax, BungeAG, Louis Dreyfus, among others. [Please see "Egypt Seeks Deal on Wheat Imports as Stocks Run Low," *Financial Times*, March 27, 2013.[262]] Ironically, while Egypt is at the precipice of its crisis, the Geneva-based Louis Dreyfus Commodities Group reported bonanza profits of over a $1 billion last year. [Please see "US Drought a Bounty for Dreyfus," *Financial Times, March 28, 2013.*[263]] Dreyfus and other commodity houses are primarily based in Switzerland, the world's leading commodities trading hub, where they are protected and contribute 3.5 percent to Switzerland's GDP. [Please see "Swiss Government Swings Behind Commodities Traders," *Financial Times, March 28, 2013.*[264]]

The United States, in turn, is the world's leading wheat producer and the world's leading wheat exporter. Rather than using this vastly important resource to be marketed in the service of the nation, in a world where food is becoming the hypercritical commodity, we are letting Swiss-based commodity traders set the ground rules of how wheat is bought and sold, all the while permitting the commodity exchanges, with their casino-inspired and government-protected investment banks, to set the prices to be paid. And all this occurs without the slightest consideration of the nation's core strategic interests, much less humanitarian concerns. (It is significant to note that the UN has predicted that, with ever-increasing populations, the world's food supply will have to increase 70 percent by 2050, a target that will be extremely difficult to achieve, given changing diets, weather conditions, depletion of mined fertilizers, such as phosphates, potash, and nitrates, plus various farming impediments, such as available water supply, population sprawl, and so on.)

The Egyptian imbroglio is a clarion call for us to restudy exactly what our objectives are, as well as what our responsibilities are as the leading exporter of grains (wheat and corn) the second-largest exporter of soybeans, and so on, as these foods are so basic to many throughout the world.

The Swiss commodity houses are business enterprises, and highly successful ones at that, along with being powerhouses in the oil-trading field, together with Vitol, the world's largest oil trader, which recently hired the grain trading team from Viterra to become a force in the grain trading arena as well.[265] But that is clearly their priority: business. Perhaps it is long past time for the United States to create its own commodity-selling entity, focusing on food/feed grains, being the world's largest food/feed grain exporter, perhaps as an arm of the Ex-Im bank, given its experience in financing offshore endeavors, with the policy guidance of the Department of State and the Department of Agriculture. Along with this new focus and responsibility, it is also high time that the nation establishes a Strategic Grain Reserve much in keeping with the Strategic Petroleum Reserve (SPR).

Dealing with Egypt's current emergency would be feasible were we to have such a structure in place. Considerations beyond the immediate ability to pay, and even price, could be held in abeyance. Perhaps it would be far more meaningful to this nation, that this young republic, in responding to one of the world's oldest civilizations in a gracious way, by being of help, but without diktat, in making our wheat available to the sixteen million Egyptian families that are sustained by the government's subsidized bread program. Certainly, there will be those in the Muslim Brotherhood so filled with hatred toward us who will continue their rhetorical fulminations. But what of the near 50 percent or more of Egyptians who risked their lives to achieve a society free to express themselves, where women would be respected and all religions would be honored. Those are the Egyptians with whom we are allied, and they are suffering enough under the current "presidency." Let us not punish them twice.

European Union's Oil Probe is Years Overdue and Targets the Wrong Benchmark

Posted: 05/16/2013, 8:04 AM EDT

The European antitrust authorities have finally carried out inspections of oil firms in three countries, as well as the offices of Platts, the price-index publisher, to determine whether the oil firms with the cognizance of Platts distorted published prices of crude oil and petroleum products. It is a long overdue first step but it targets the wrong benchmark.

Platts serves as a guidepost for the real-time pricing of physical product. Factors such as grade and port of loading can have a wide impact on the nuances of day-to-day pricing differences. Yet their impact on the oil trade's pricing structure is marginal at best.

Benchmarks such as Brent crude and West Texas Intermediate (WTI) determine the core world-traded price of oil on the commodity exchanges, the prices that reflect the financialization of commodity prices worldwide. The prices quoted on the exchanges for oil and oil products lend themselves to vast distortion, in tens of dollars per barrel and near billions of dollars on a daily basis worldwide, through speculation if not outright manipulation. These prices have left all vestige of supply and demand. Over 70 percent of the trading on the exchanges is done not by producers or users hedging their production or consumption needs, but by speculators and traders who neither produce nor consume the oil they trade through the exchanges. As a grim example of the dimension of the issue at hand, the April 19, 2013 *Wall Street Journal* article "Traders Slip on Brent Oil Bet"[266] reported that the Brent futures contracts alone, held by "investors" on March 8, 2013, was a record 1.58 million contracts. Consider each contract represents 1,000 barrels of oil. The world's daily consumption of oil is some 85 million barrels. You do the math.

This corner has tried to bring light to this issue through a series of past posts particularly the following:

- "Commodity Exchanges Prime the Pump for Higher Oil/ Gasoline Prices" (May 31, 2012)[267]

- "Oil Prices Skyrocket 9.36 Percent in Friday's Trading. Supply and Demand, Eh?" (July 2, 2012)[268]

- "Are Our Leaders Hearing ExxonMobil CEO Tillerson" (May 7, 2011)[269]

- "Oil Speculation at Chevron Laid Bare for All to See" (July 20, 2011)[270]

- "BP's Smoking Gun and the Manipulation of Oil Prices" (June 30, 2010)[271]

- "The Trade That Brought Us $100/barrel Oil Teaches Us to Be Afraid, Very Afraid" (January 7, 2008)[272]

We can only hope that the European Authority's probe is the first step and extends not only to oil companies but to active oil traders such as the bank holding companies Morgan Stanley, JPMorgan Chase, Goldman Sachs, and others as well as the trading desks of the varied oil companies themselves as well as the trading houses active in the field such as Glencore, Vitol, et al to determine for whom the trades are made, and to what avail.

CONCLUSION

As per my previous writings, this book has tried to be a clarion call to the massive distortion of oil prices orchestrated by big and little oil, the casino bank holding companies and their massive financial girth, the traders using under-regulated exchanges and their enablers in our government and its inept agencies, the manipulations of the OPEC cartel and its laissez-passer extended by our courts and Department of Justice, and a somnolent media, all of whom preside over one of the great thefts of wealth in human history.

We are robbed of billions of dollars every day by oil interests, in their manipulation of the market pricing mechanisms, at massive cost and risk to the world's economy. Here, too, as I have tried to point out, Wall Street and the significant resources of the financial sector and its access to beneficent government funding play a key role in the distortion of the oil market through vast speculation that is virtually unhindered by government oversight agencies.

Oil is the lifeblood of many Middle East autocracies, and as touched upon herein, oil is also the lifeblood of terrorism. Any attempt to weaken oil's stranglehold on our economy, the environment, our national security, and so on, is treated by oil's beneficiaries as an act of aggression and immediately targeted by powerful oil interests and their hangers-on, both domestic and foreign.

This book has tried to point out, once again, where the money goes, asking, *cui bono?* That is, who benefits? Ignorance of how oil prices and policies are manipulated is the greatest asset and greatest tool of the oil industry and its allies. It is essential that Americans and oil consumers throughout the world understand where the money they pay for petroleum products goes—including the money they pay at the pump, the money they pay to heat their homes, and the money they pay for the vast universe of other petroleum-based products. And not just *where* the money goes, but also *why*. Only then will those responsible for policy act in the interest of the common good, and not simply for their friends and lobbyists from the universal "oil patch."

NOTES

[**AUTHOR'S NOTE:** *All links and reference data that appear in this section can be accessed at www.RaymondLearsy.com/links. Glossary terms pertinent to the text can be accessed at www. RaymondLearsy.com/glossary.*]

1. Robert A. Rankin, "Oil Regulators and Critics Clash in Senate Testimony," Philly.com, November 2, 1990, http://articles.philly.com/1990-11-02/business/25926157_1_oil-prices-crude-philip-k-verleger.

2. Senator Maria Cantwell, "Under Questioning by Cantwell, Exxon CEO Estimate Oil Should Cost $60–$70 Per Barrel," YouTube, accessed April 29, 2013, http://www.youtube.com/watch?v=LY420_U4U0I.

3. Diane Cardwell and Rick Gladstone, "Oil Prices Predicted to Stay Above $100 a Barrel Through Next Year," *New York Times*, December 28, 2011, http://www.nytimes.com/2011/12/29/business/oil-prices-predicted-to-remain-above-100-a-barrel-next-year.html?pagewanted=all&_r=0.

4. Raymond Learsy, "Time to Dismiss the CFTC Chairman and His Commissioners," *Huffington Post* (blog), December 27,

2010, http://www.huffingtonpost.com/raymond-j-learsy/oil-over-90barrel--time-t_b_801451.html.

5. Raymond Learsy, "Are Our Leaders Hearing ExxonMobil CEO Tillerson?," *Huffington Post* (blog), May 17, 2011, http://www.huffingtonpost.com/raymond-j-learsy/attorney-general-holdercf_b_862873.html.

6. Raymond Learsy, "The *New York Times* Flays Natural Gas, to the Cheers of the Oil Industry, OPEC, and Coal Producers," *Huffington Post* (blog), June 28, 2011, http://www.huffingtonpost.com/raymond-j-learsy/the-nytimes-flays-natural_b_886234.html.

7. Ian Urbina, "Insiders Sound an Alarm amid a Natural Gas Rush," *New York Times*, June 25, 2011, http://www.nytimes.com/2011/06/26/us/26gas.html?pagewanted=all.

8. Ian Urbina, "Behind Veneer, Doubt on Future of Natural Gas," *New York Times*, Jun. 26, 2011, http://www.nytimes.com/2011/06/27/us/27gas.html?pagewanted=all.

9. Raymond Learsy, "The Goldman Sachs Settlement, the *Wall Street Journal*, Warren Buffett, and the White House," *Huffington Post* (blog), July 17, 2010, http://www.huffingtonpost.com/raymond-j-learsy/the-new-york-times-contin_b_508122.html.

10. Raymond Learsy, "The *New York Times* Flays Natural Gas, to the Cheers of the Oil Industry, OPEC, and Coal Producers," *Huffington Post* (blog), June 28, 2011, http://www.huffingtonpost.com/raymond-j-learsy/the-goldman-sachs-settlem_b_650165.html.

11. *US SEC v. Citigroup Global Markets, Inc.,* Case 1:11-cv-07387-JSR Document 33 Filed 11/28/11, Filed Nov. 28, 2011, http://online. wsj.com/public/resources/documents/SECCITI11282011.pdf.

12. <u>Raymond Learsy, "OPEC's 'Noble Cause,'" *Huffington Post* (blog), December 17, 2008,</u> http://www.huffingtonpost.com/ raymond-j-learsy/opecs-noble-cause_b_151961.html.

13. Javier Blas and Guy Chazan, "Saudi Arabia Targets $100 Crude Price," *Financial Times,* January 16, 2012, http://www.ft.com/ intl/cms/s/0/af13f09c-405f-11e1-9bce-00144feab49a.html.

14. "What is CNG?," http://www.cngnow.com/what-is-cng/Pages/ default.aspx.

15. Rick Gladstone and J. David Goodman, "Iran Says It May Cut Off Its Oil Exports to Europe," *New York Times,* January 26, 2012, http://www.nytimes.com/2012/01/27/world/middleeast/ ahmadinejad-says-iran-is-ready-for-nuclear-talks.html?_r=0.

16. Ibid.

17. <u>Raymond Learsy, "Iran's Oil Threat, 'Déjà vu, All Over Again,'" *Huffington Post* (blog), January 30, 2012,</u> http://www. huffingtonpost.com/raymond-j-learsy/irans-oil-threat-deja-vu_b_1240948.html.

18. CNN wire staff, "Oil Minister: Saudi Arabia Can Make Up for Iranian Crude," CNN, January 17, 2012, http://www.cnn. com/2012/01/16/world/meast/saudi-oil-production.

19. <u>Dan Barry, "In Fuel Oil Country, Cold That Cuts to the Heart," *New York Times,* February 3, 2012,</u> http://www.nytimes. com/2012/02/04/us/maine-resident-struggles-to-heat-his-home.html.

20. Raymond Learsy, "Obama Administration Announces Formation of Oil/Gas Pricing Fraud Panel. Really?," *Huffington Post* (blog), April, 27, 2011, http://www.huffingtonpost.com/raymond-j-learsy/obama-administration-anno_b_854190.html.

21. Raymond Learsy, "The Half-Billion Solyndra Debacle—Why Is Steven Chu Energy Secretary?," *Huffington Post* (blog), September, 26, 2011, http://www.huffingtonpost.com/raymond-j-learsy/the-half-billion-solyndra_b_981325.html.

22. Raymond Learsy, "Time to Dismiss the CFTC Chairman and His Commissioners," *Huffington Post* (blog), December 27, 2010, http://www.huffingtonpost.com/raymond-j-learsy/oil-over-90barrel--time-t_b_801451.html.

23. Ben Protess and Peter Eavis, "At Volcker Rule Deadline, a Strong Pushback from Wall St.," *New York Times,* February 13, 2012, http://dealbook.nytimes.com/2012/02/13/at-volcker-rule-deadline-a-strong-pushback-from-wall-st/.

24. Andrew Ross Sorkin, "The Volcker Rule and the Costs of Good Intentions," *New York Times,* February 13, 2012, http://dealbook.nytimes.com/2012/02/13/the-volcker-rule-and-the-costs-of-good-intentions/.

25. Paul A. Volcker, "Commentary on the Restrictions on Proprietary Trading by Insured Depositary Institutions," *Wall Street Journal,* http://online.wsj.com/public/resources/documents/Volcker_Rule_Essay_2-13-12.pdf.

26. Andrew Ross Sorkin, "One Crowd Still Loyal to Goldman Sachs," *New York Times,* June 14, 2010, http://www.nytimes.com/2010/06/15/business/15sorkin.html.

27. Andrew E. Kramer, "An Embargo and a Boon," *New York Times*, February 16, 2012, http://www.nytimes.com/2012/02/17/business/global/russian-oil-industry-set-to-capitalize-if-embargo-hits-iran.html.

28. Raymond Learsy, "The Trade That Brought Us $100/ barrel Oil Teaches Us to Be Afraid, Be Very Afraid," *Huffington Post* (blog), January, 7, 2008, http://www.huffingtonpost.com/raymond-j-learsy/the-trade-that-brought-us_1_b_80149.html.

29. James Quinn, "US Oil Speculators Fined for $100-a-Barrel 'Vanity Trade,'" *Telegraph*, August 18, 2010, http://www.telegraph.co.uk/finance/newsbysector/energy/oilandgas/7950879/US-oil-speculators-fined-for-100-a-barrel-vanity-trade.html.

30. Andrew E. Kramer, "An Embargo and a Boon," *New York Times*, February 16, 2012, http://www.nytimes.com/2012/02/17/business/global/russian-oil-industry-set-to-capitalize-if-embargo-hits-iran.html.

31. Jean Eaglesham, Paul Vieira, and David Enrich, "Traders Manipulated Key Rate, Banks Say," *Wall Street Journal*, February 17, 2012, http://online.wsj.com/article/SB10001424052970204059804577227452963906044.html.

32. Emiko Terazono, "Swiss Review Supports Commodities Trading," *Financial Times*, March 27, 2013, http://www.ft.com/intl/cms/s/0/f110aa02-96ef-11e2-a77c-00144feabdc0.html#axzz2ROtLgIDh.

33. Javier Blas, "Vitol Expands into Grains Trading," *Financial Times*, April 2, 2013, http://www.ft.com/cms/s/0/af3a4468-9bad-11e2-a820-00144feabdc0.html#axzz2ROPyvmjK.

34. Dan Berman, "Obama Administration Taps Strategic Petroleum Reserve," *Politico Pro*, June 23, 2011, http://www.politico.com/news/stories/0611/57620.html.

35. John Boehner, "Congressman Boehner Statement on Administration Plans to Open the Strategic Petroleum Reserve," press release, June 23, 2011, http://johnboehner.house.gov/News/DocumentSingle.aspx?DocumentID=248394.

36. CME Group website, http://www.cmegroup.com/.

37. Jacob Bunge, "CFTC Suit Marks New Era," *Wall Street Journal*, February 24, 2013, http://online.wsj.com/article/SB1000142412 78873236997045783245600483047222.html.

38. Raymond Learsy, "Time to Dismiss the CFTC Chairman and His Commissioners," *Huffington Post* (blog), December 27, 2010, http://www.huffingtonpost.com/raymond-j-learsy/oil-over-90barrel--time-t_b_801451.html.

39. Raymond Learsy, "Obama Administration Announces Formation of Oil/Gas Pricing Fraud Panel. Really?," *Huffington Post* (blog), April 27, 2011, http://www.huffingtonpost.com/raymond-j-learsy/obama-administration-anno_b_854190.html.

40. CME Group, "CME Group Announced Record Energy Trading Volumes," earnings releases and financial reports, New York, February 8, 2012, http://investor.cmegroup.com/investor-relations/releasedetail.cfm?ReleaseID=647364.

41. Barack Obama, Weekly Address, The White House, March 3, 2012, *whitehouse.gov*, http://www.whitehouse.gov/the-press-office/2012/03/03/weekly-address-taking-control-our-energy-future.

42. Barack Obama, press conference, The White House, March 6, 2012, *whitehouse.gov,* http://www.whitehouse.gov/the-press-office/2012/03/06/press-conference-president.

43. Ibid.

44. Barack Obama, "Remarks by the President on Fair Trade," The White House, Rose Garden, March 13, 2012, *whitehouse. gov,* http://www.whitehouse.gov/the-press-office/2012/03/13/remarks-president-fair-trade.

45. Summer Said, "Saudi Arabia Reluctant to Replace Iran Oil," *Wall Street Journal,* March 12, 2012, http://online.wsj.com/article/SB10001424052702304537904577277301694700334.html.

46. Chris Baltimore, "Senate Okays Plan to Sue OPEC for Price-Fixing," Reuters, June 19, 2007, http://www.reuters.com/article/2007/06/19/us-usa-energy-senate-opec-idUSN1919767120070619.

47. Raymond Learsy, "Oil: A Defining Moment for Our Political Class and the Press," *Huffington Post* (blog), July 9, 2007, http://www.huffingtonpost.com/raymond-j-learsy/oil-a-defining-moment-for_b_55363.html.

48. Energy Policy Research Foundation, Inc., *epring.org,* http://eprinc.org/about-us/.

49. Alex Guillen, "Chu: DOE Working to Wean US off Oil," *Politico Pro,* February 28, 2012, http://www.politico.com/news/stories/0212/73408.html.

50. Neil King, Jr. and Stephen Power, "Times Tough for Energy Overhaul," *Wall Street Journal,* December 12, 2008, http://online.wsj.com/article/SB122904040307499791.html.

51. Barack Obama, "Remarks by the President on American-Made Energy," Cushing Pipe Yard, Cushing, Oklahoma, March 22, 2012, *whitehouse.gov,* http://www.whitehouse.gov/the-press-office/2012/03/22/remarks-president-american-made-energy.

52. Luciana Juvenal and Ivan Petrella, "Speculation in the Oil Market," *Economic Synopses,* Federal Reserve Bank of St. Louis, 2012, no. 8, posted on March 13, 2012, http://research.stlouisfed.org/publications/es/12/ES_2012-03-12.pdf.

53. Raymond Learsy, "Obama Fulminates over China's Export Restrictions on Rare-Earths While Silent on OPEC's Collusion," *Huffington Post* (blog), March 18, 2012, http://www.huffingtonpost.com/raymond-j-learsy/obama-opec_b_1358919.html.

54. Raymond Learsy, "Oil Embargoes, Sherlock Holmes, and the Russian Butler," *Huffington Post* (blog), February 20, 2012, http://www.huffingtonpost.com/raymond-j-learsy/oil-embargoessherlock-hol_b_1288687.html.

55. Ali al-Naimi, "Saudi Arabia Will Act to Lower Soaring Oil Prices," *Financial Times,* March 28, 2012, http://www.ft.com/intl/cms/s/0/9e1ccb48-781c-11e1-b237-00144feab49a.html#axzz1qb9f034m.

56. William Maclean and Barbara Lewis, "OPEC Makes Deepest Oil Cut Ever to Rescue Prices," Reuters, December 17, 2008, http://www.reuters.com/article/2008/12/17/us-opec-idUSLG66045920081217.

57. Ali al-Naimi, "Saudi Oil Policy: Stability with Strength," speech in Houston, Texas, October 20, 1999, http://www.saudiembassy.net/archive/1999/speeches/page4.aspx.

58. Raymond Learsy, "'Noble' OPEC Criticizes the International Energy Agency," *Huffington Post* (blog), January 19, 2011, http://www.huffingtonpost.com/raymond-j-learsy/noble-opec-criticzes-the_b_810810.html.

59. Steve Stecklow, Spencer Swartz, and Margaret Coker, "Oil Trade With Iran Thrives, Discreetly," *Wall Street Journal,* May 20, 2010, http://online.wsj.com/article/SB100014240527487036 91804575254554231664686.html?mg=id-wsj.

60. Richard Mably and Peg Mackey, "Exclusive: Shell Scrambles to Pay Huge Bill for Iran Oil," Reuters, March 25, 2012, http://www.reuters.com/article/2012/03/25/us-shell-iran-idUSBRE82O07420120325.

61. "Death of Neda Agha-Soltan," *Wikipedia,* http://en.wikipedia.org/wiki/Death_of_Neda_Agha-Soltan.

62. Raymond Learsy, "The Volcker Rule and Wall Street's Pliant Media Plant," *Huffington Post* (blog), February 15, 2012, http://www.huffingtonpost.com/raymond-j-learsy/the-volcker-rule-and-wall_b_1278419.html.

63. Andrew Ross Sorkin, "For Gates-Like Wealth, Look Beyond Wall Street," *New York Times,* April 4, 2012, http://dealbook.nytimes.com/2012/04/04/for-gates-like-wealth-look-beyond-wall-street/.

64. Julie Creswell and Azam Ahmed, "Large Hedge Funds Fared Well in 2011," *New York Times,* March 29, 2012, http://dealbook.nytimes.com/2012/03/29/large-hedge-funds-fared-well-in-2011/.

65. Jad Mouawad, "Fuel to Burn: Now What?," *New York Times,* April 10, 2012, http://www.nytimes.com/2012/04/11/business/

energy-environment/energy-boom-in-us-upends-expectations.
html?pagewanted=all&_r=0.

66. John M. Broder, "An Inconvenient Statement, Retracted," *New York Times* (blog), March 13, 2012, http://green.blogs.nytimes.com/2012/03/13/an-inconvenient-statement-retracted/?gwh=3A3B229E62B88BCDEFC1655A9EE1092A.

67. Alex Guillen, "Obama Energy Chief Bombshell Admission …," Fox News, February 29, 2012, http://nation.foxnews.com/steven-chu/2012/02/29/obama-energy-chief-bombshell-admission.

68. The *New York Times* is presently having difficulty posting the 2012 conference. They replaced the link with the 2013 conference videos; however, we have been told that they are working on it. http://www.livestream.com/nytenergyfortomorrow?utm_source=lsplayer&utm_medium=embed&utm_campaign=footerlinks.

69. Barack Obama, "President Obama Speaks on Increasing Oversight on Manipulation in the Oil Market," The White House, April 17, 2012, *whitehouse.gov,* http://www.whitehouse.gov/photos-and-video/video/2012/04/17/president-obama-speaks-increasing-oversight-manipulation-oil-market.

70. "CME Group Statement Regarding White House Proposal to Increase Oversight of Energy Markets," CME Group, Inc., accessed April 30, 2013, http://investor.cmegroup.com/investor-relations/releasedetail.cfm?ReleaseID=664996.

71. David Sheppard, "Obama Oil Margin Plan Could Increase Price Swings," Reuters, April 20, 2012, http://www.reuters.com/article/2012/04/20/us-obama-cftc-margins-idUSBRE83I1FO20120420.

72. Robert A. Rankin, "Oil Regulators and Critics Clash In Senate Testimony," *Philly.com,* November 2. 1990, http://articles.philly.com/1990-11-02/business/25926157_1_oil-prices-crude-philip-k-verleger.

73. "CFTC Scores 'Milestone' Win on Oil-Price Manipulation," *Chicago Tribune,* April 20, 2012, http://articles.chicagotribune.com/2012-04-20/business/chi-cftc-scores-milestone-win-on-oilprice-manipulation-20120420_1_oil-price-manipulation-oil-prices-oil-futures.

74. Reuters, "UPDATE 2-High-Frequency Trader Optiver Pays $14 Million over Oil Manipulation," *Chicago Tribune,* April 19, 2012, http://articles.chicagotribune.com/2012-04-19/news/sns-rt-optiversettlement-update-2l2e8fjip8-20120419_1_oil-market-manipulation-oil-prices-high-frequency-trading.

75. David Sheppard, "Obama Oil Margin Plan Could Increase Price Swings," Reuters, April 19, 2012, http://www.reuters.com/article/2012/04/19/us-obama-cftc-margins-idUSBRE83I1FO20120419.

76. First on CNBC interview, "Pickens on Chesapeake Energy," CNBC (video), April 30, 2012, accessed April 30, 2013, http://video.cnbc.com/gallery/?video=3000087359.

77. John Collins Rudolf, "Leaked Cables Reveal US Concerns Over Saudi 'Peak Oil,'" *New York Times* (blog), February 10, 2011, http://green.blogs.nytimes.com/2011/02/10/leaked-cables-reveal-u-s-concerns-over-saudi-peak-oil/.

78. Jad Mouawad, "Oil Innovations Pump New Life into Old Wells," *New York Times,* March 5, 2007, correction March 6, 2007, accessed April 30, 2013, http://www.nytimes.com/2007/03/05/business/05oil1.html?pagewanted=all.

79. Susannah Snider, "Gas Prices around the World," *Kiplinger,* March 31, 2011, http://www.kiplinger.com/article/cars/T009-C000-S001-gas-prices-around-the-world.html.

80. Dan Berman and Byron Tau, "T. Boone Pickens Visited White House Seven Times," *Politico,* January 26, 2012, http://www.politico.com/news/stories/0112/72041.html.

81. Clifford Krauss, "Chesapeake's Chief Executive Addresses Disclosures," *New York Times,* May 2, 2012, http://www.nytimes.com/2012/05/03/business/energy-environment/chesapeakes-chief-executive-addresses-disclosures.html.

82. Joshua Schneyer and Brian Grow, "Special Report: Energy Giant Hid behind Shells In 'Land Grab,'" Reuters, December 28, 2011, http://www.reuters.com/article/2011/12/28/us-energy-giant-idUSTRE7BR0G420111228.

83. Raymond Learsy, "Oil Speculation At Chevron Laid Bare for All to See," *Huffington Post* (blog), July 20, 2011, http://www.huffingtonpost.com/raymond-j-learsy/oil-speculation-at-chevro_b_904289.html.

84. Raymond Learsy, "JPMorgan Chase Banks on Buying Into the Casino," *Huffington Post* (blog), November 25, 2011, http://www.huffingtonpost.com/raymond-j-learsy/jpmorgan-chase-banks-on-b_b_1112835.html.

85. Lee Fang, "JPMorgan, Koch, Other Oil Traders May Buy Discounted Strategic Petroleum Reserve Oil and Simply Store It," *Climate Progress,* July 5, 2011, accessed April 30, 2013, http://thinkprogress.org/climate/2011/07/05/260732/oil-barons-may-store-spr-oil/?mobile=nc.

86. "The Dimon Principle," Wall Street Journal, May 15, 2012, http://online.wsj.com/article/SB10001424052702304371504574 02331446053716.html?mod=googlenews_wsj.

87. Dan Fitzpatrick and Carolyn Cui, "JPMorgan Commodities Chief Takes the Heat," *Wall Street Journal,* October 9, 2010, http://online.wsj.com/article/SB10001424052748703927504575 5540241298913962.html.

88. Raymond Learsy, "Bravo JPMorgan! Just What We Need, Another Wall Street Casino," *Huffington Post* (blog), October 12, 2010, http://www.huffingtonpost.com/raymond-j-learsy/ bravo-jp-morgan-just-what_b_759262.html.

89. Raymond Learsy, "JPMorgan Chase Banks on Buying Into the Casino," *Huffington Post* (blog), November 25, 2011, http:// www.huffingtonpost.com/raymond-j-learsy/jpmorgan-chase-banks-on-b_b_1112835.html.

90. Stephanie Ruhle, Bradley Keoun, and Mary Childes, "JPMorgan Trader's Position Said to Distort Credit Indexes," *Bloomberg,* April 6, 2012, http://www.bloomberg.com/news/2012-04-05/ jpmorgan-trader-iksil-s-heft-is-said-to-distort-credit-indexes. html.

91. Monica Langley, "Inside JPMorgan's Blunder," *Wall Street Journal,* May 18, 2012, http://online.wsj.com/article/SB100014 24052702303448404577410341236847980.html.

92. Raymond Learsy, "Are Our Leaders Hearing ExxonMobil CEO Tillerson?," *Huffington Post* (blog), May 17, 2011, http:// www.huffingtonpost.com/raymond-j-learsy/attorney-general-holdercf_b_862873.html.

93. Raymond Learsy, "America Needs a President Who Will Confront the Financial Industry's Hegemony over Our Lives," *Huffington Post* (blog), July 14, 2011, http://www.huffingtonpost.com/raymond-j-learsy/america-needs-a-president_b_898047.html.

94. CNBC exclusive, "Sheila Bair: Break Up JPMorgan," CNBC (video), http://video.cnbc.com/gallery/?video=3000092555.

95. Reuters, "CME Group Attacks White House Plan on Oil Margins," Reuters, April 17, 2012, http://www.reuters.com/article/2012/04/17/cme-margins-whitehouse-idUSL2E8FHBNJ20120417.

96. Raymond Learsy, "President Obama Speaks, and the Oil Speculators React," *Huffington Post* (blog), April 24, 2012, http://www.huffingtonpost.com/raymond-j-learsy/president-obama-speaks-an_b_1448280.html.

97. Raymond Learsy, "Does JPMorgan's Derivatives Fiasco Portend the Collapse of Crude Oil and Gasoline Prices?," *Huffington Post* (blog), May 21, 2012, http://www.huffingtonpost.com/raymond-j-learsy/does-jpmorgans-derivative_b_1532538.html.

98. Terence P. Jeffrey, "GAO: Recoverable Oil in Colorado, Utah, Wyoming 'About Equal to Entire World's Proven Oil Reserves,'" CNS News, May 11, 2012, http://cnsnews.com/news/article/gao-recoverable-oil-colorado-utah-wyoming-about-equal-entire-world-s-proven-oil.

99. Ayesha Daya, "Saudi Arabia Achieving $100 Oil Signals Output Reversal," *Bloomberg Businessweek*, June 7, 2012, http://www.businessweek.com/news/2012-06-06/saudi-arabia-achieving-100-oil-signals-output-reversal.

100. Steve Liesman, "How Jamie Dimon Wiffed on the Volcker Rule," CNBC, June 13, 2012, http://www.cnbc.com/id/47803236.

101. Editorial, "JPMorgan Chase's $2 Billion Loss," *New York Times*, May 11, 2012, http://www.nytimes.com/2012/05/12/opinion/jpmorgan-chases-2-billion-loss.html.

102. Dan Fitzpatrick and Carolyn Cui, "JPMorgan Commodities Chief Takes the Heat," *Wall Street Journal*, October 9, 2010, http://online.wsj.com/article/SB10001424052748703927504575540241298913962.html.

103. Mark Scott and Michael J. De La Merced, "JPMorgan Said to Buy MF Global Stake in London Metal Exchange," *New York Times*, November 23, 2011, http://dealbook.nytimes.com/2011/11/23/jpmorgan-said-to-buy-mf-global-stake-in-london-metal-exchange/.

104. Ikuko Kurahone, London; Osamu Tsukimori, Tokyo, "JPMorgan Hires ex-Goldman Energy Trader in Asia," Reuters, June 12, 2012, http://www.reuters.com/article/2012/06/12/us-jpmorgan-hiring-energy-idUSBRE85B0AJ20120612.

105. Jonathan Saul, "JPMorgan Hires Crude Tanker to Store Gasoil-Trade," Reuters, June 3, 2009, http://www.reuters.com/article/2009/06/03/energy-products-storage-idUSL365078320090603.

106. Louise Armistead and Rowena Mason, "JPMorgan Revealed as Mystery Trader That Bought £1 Billion-Worth of Copper on LME," *Telegraph*, December 04, 2010, http://www.telegraph.co.uk/finance/newsbysector/industry/8180304/JP-Morgan-revealed-as-mystery-trader-that-bought-1bn-worth-of-copper-on-LME.html.

107. Samuel R. Avro, "Energy Secretary Admits to Naiveté Over OPEC Remarks," *Energy Trends Insider,* February 19, 2009, http://www.energytrendsinsider.com/2009/02/19/energy-secretary-admits-naivete-over-opec-remarks/.

108. Edmund L. Andrews, "Reluctant Iran Falls in Line With OPEC Production Rise," *New York Times,* March 30, 2000, http://www.nytimes.com/2000/03/30/world/reluctant-iran-falls-in-line-with-opec-production-rise.html?src=pm.

109. John M. Broder, "An Inconvenient Statement, Retracted," *New York Times* (blog), March 13, 2012, http://green.blogs.nytimes.com/2012/03/13/an-inconvenient-statement-retracted/.

110. John Boehner, "Is Addressing High Gas Prices a Goal for the Obama Admin? 'No,'" Speaker of the House online, February 29, 2012, http://www.speaker.gov/general/addressing-high-gas-prices-goal-obama-admin-%E2%80%9Cno%E2%80%9D.

111. Alexandros Pertsinidis, Yunxiang Zhang, and Steven Chu, "Subnanometre Single-Molecule Localization, Registration and Distance Measurements," *Nature,* 466, 647–651, July 29, 2010, published online July 7, 2010, http://www.nature.com/nature/journal/v466/n7306/abs/nature09163.html.

112. Matthew L. Wald, "Energy Department Steps In to Help Uranium Enrichment Company," *New York Times,* June 13, 2012, http://www.nytimes.com/2012/06/14/science/earth/energy-department-steps-in-to-help-uranium-enrichment-company.html?_r=1&.

113. BBC News Middle East, "Iran Nuclear Talks in Moscow 'Yield No Breakthrough,'" June 18, 2012, http://www.bbc.co.uk/news/world-middle-east-18481827.

114. Edmund L. Andrews, "Greenspan Concedes Error on Regulation," *New York Times,* October 23, 2008, http://www.nytimes.com/2008/10/24/business/economy/24panel.html?_r=0.

115. "Greenspan: US Economy Looks 'Very Sluggish,'" *Bloomberg,* June 21, 2012, http://www.bloomberg.com/video/95061517-greenspan-u-s-economy-looks-very-sluggish.html.

116. Raymond Learsy, "Peak Oil Is Snake Oil!," *Huffington Post* (blog), June 25, 2007, http://www.huffingtonpost.com/raymond-j-learsy/peak-oil-is-snake-oil_b_53546.html.

117. Leonardo Maugeri, "The Geopolitics of Energy Project: Oil: The Next Revolution," Harvard Kennedy School, Belfer Center, (Cambridge, MA, 2012), http://belfercenter.ksg.harvard.edu/files/Oil- The Next Revolution.pdf.

118. Raymond Learsy, "$33 Barrel Oil Now and Forever. With Leadership!," *Huffington Post* (blog), June 3, 2012, http://www.huffingtonpost.com/raymond-j-learsy/33-barrel-oil-now-and-for_b_1565997.html.

119. Raymond Learsy, "Energy Independence, Our Oil Shale Deposits, Making OPEC Obsolete," *Huffington Post* (blog), October 13, 2006, http://www.huffingtonpost.com/raymond-j-learsy/energy-independence-our-o_b_31608.html.

120. Raymond Learsy, "Are Our Leaders Hearing ExxonMobil CEO Tillerson?," *Huffington Post* (blog), May 17, 2011, http://www.huffingtonpost.com/raymond-j-learsy/attorney-general-holdercf_b_862873.html.

121. Leonardo Maugeri, "The Geopolitics of Energy Project: Oil: The Next Revolution," Harvard Kennedy School, Belfer Center,

(Cambridge, MA, 2012), http://belfercenter.ksg.harvard.edu/files/Oil-%20The%20Next%20Revolution.pdf.

122. Reuters, "REFILE-UPDATE 7—Barclays Paying $453 Million to Settle LIBOR Probe," June 28, 2012, http://in.reuters.com/article/2012/06/28/barclays-libor-idINL6E8HRA5320120628.

123. Alexandra Alper and Kirstin Ridley, "Barclays Paying $453 Million to Settle LIBOR probe," Reuters, June 27, 2012, http://www.reuters.com/article/2012/06/27/us-barclays-libor-idUSBRE85Q0J720120627.

124. Antoine Gara, "Barclays Fine Signals Fraud in $350 Trillion Lending Market (UPDATE 1)," *The Street* online, June 27, 2012, http://www.thestreet.com/story/11598878/2/barclays-fine-signals-fraud-in-350-trillion-lending-market.html.

125. Andrew E. Kramer and David M. Herszenhorn, "Former Russian Minister Warns of Economic Ebb," *New York Times,* June 23, 2012, http://www.nytimes.com/2012/06/24/world/europe/former-russian-finance-minister-warns-of-recession.html.

126. Edward Wyatt, "Ex-ConAgra Unit Settles With US Over Artificial Oil Trade," *New York Times,* August 16, 2010, http://www.nytimes.com/2010/08/17/business/17ftc.html?adxnnl=1&adxnnlx=1364407945-c+Qpy4DOP465k1d1g2VoPg&gwh=F7380873FB95A1AC1FBE764F88E3B9D3.

127. "Stocks: Best Day of Year for S&P 500 as Europe Talks Unity," *USA Today,* Money, June 29, 2012, http://usatoday30.usatoday.com/money/markets/story/2012-06-29/stocks-june-29/55911078/1.

128. "A Fracking Rule Reprieve," *Wall Street Journal*, June 29, 2012, http://online.wsj.com/article/SB10001424052702304870304577490680003198686.html.

129. Peter Orszag, "Natural Gas Cars Can Drive Us toward a Better Economy," *Bloomberg*, June 26, 2012, http://www.bloomberg.com/news/2012-06-26/natural-gas-cars-can-drive-us-toward-a-better-economy.html.

130. Justin Menza, "JPMorgan's Dimon Deserves Clawback: Bair," CNBC, July 11, 2012, http://www.cnbc.com/id/48147653.

131. Constantine Von Hoffman, "Sheila Bair's FDIC Was Hated by Wall Street—And That's High Praise Indeed," CBS News, Moneywatch, July 15, 2011, http://www.cbsnews.com/8301-505123_162-49640965/sheila-bairs-fdic-was-hated-by-wall-street----and-thats-high-praise-indeed/.

132. Raymond Learsy, "The Jamie Dimon 'Puppet Show,'" *Huffington Post* (blog), June 14, 2012, http://www.huffingtonpost.com/raymond-j-learsy/the-jamie-dimon-puppet-sh_b_1596675.html.

133. Raymond Learsy, "It's All about the Money: Jamie Dimon's Big Pay Hike and the Home Foreclosures of Our Servicemen,'" *Huffington Post* (blog), February 19, 2011, http://www.huffingtonpost.com/raymond-j-learsy/its-all-about-the-money-j_b_825485.html.

134. BBC News, "Diamond to 'Forgo' £20 Million Bonus amid LIBOR Scandal," July 10, 2012, http://www.bbc.co.uk/news/business-18781509.

135. "Under Questioning by Cantwell, Exxon CEO Estimates Oil Should Cost $60-70 Per Barrel," *YouTube* (video), May 12, 2011

(when questioned by US Senator Maria Cantwell (D-WA) at a Senate Finance Committee hearing), http://www.youtube. com/watch?v=LY420_U4U0I.

136. US Commodity Futures Trading Commission, speeches and testimony, "Speculators and Commodity Prices—Redux," Commissioner Bart Chilton, February 24, 2012, http://cftc.gov/ PressRoom/SpeechesTestimony/chiltonstatement022412.

137. Gregory Meyer, "Wall Street Bankers Step Up Oil Trade Role," *Financial Times,* July 15, 2012, http://www.ft.com/ intl/cms/s/0/96c4dd5e-ce70-11e1-9fa7-00144feabdc0. html#axzz20y8jcqNn.

138. Raymond Learsy, "Your TARP Money is Being Used to Prop Up the Price of Oil," *The Huffington Post* (blog), January 23, 2009, http://www.huffingtonpost.com/raymond-j-learsy/your-tarp-money-being-use_b_160249.html.

139. Raymond Learsy, "Is JPMorgan a Bank or a Government-Funded Casino?," *Huffington Post* (blog), June 9, 2009, http:// www.huffingtonpost.com/raymond-j-learsy/is-jp-morgan-a-bank-or-a_b_212971.html.

140. Josephine Mason, "Goldman Sachs Expands Physical Base Metals Team," Reuters, July 19, 2012, http://in.reuters. com/article/2012/07/18/goldman-metals-appointment-idINL2E8IIA8320120718.

141. Raymond Learsy, "Banks in Collusion With the Fed Shamelessly Spike Up Price of Oil/Gasoline," *Huffington Post* (blog), July 18, 2012, http://www.huffingtonpost.com/raymond-j-learsy/the-banks-in-collusion-wi_b_1681685.html.

142. Raymond Learsy, "JP Morgan Chase Banks on Buying Into the Casino," *Huffington Post* (blog), November 25, 2011, http://www.huffingtonpost.com/raymond-j-learsy/jpmorgan-chase-banks-on-b_b_1112835.html.

143. Jack Farchly and Gregory Meyer, "World Braced for New Food Crisis," *Financial Times*, July 19, 2012, http://www.ft.com/intl/cms/s/2/9989dc80-d1c5-11e1-badb-00144feabdc0.html#axzz2OqUUHVhu.

144. Marshall Eckblad, "Drought Dries Up Cattle Market," *The Wall Street Journal*, August 1, 2012, http://online.wsj.com/article/SB10000872396390044354550457756324188362730.html?cb=logged0.7770966439648059.

145. Mekong Oryza, "PM Looks to Counter OPEC, Push Rice-Exporting Power," Jul. 19, 2012, http://mekongoryza.com/news/local-news/244/pm-looks-to-counter-opec-push-rice-exporting-power.html.

146. Jack Farchy, "Hedge Funds Bet on Corn Prices to Soar," *Financial Times*, August 1, 2012, http://www.ft.com/intl/cms/s/0/3170d198-dbf8-11e1-86f8-00144feab49a.html#axzz2OqUUHVhu.

147. Liz Alderman, "Indigestion for 'les Riches' in a Plan for Higher Taxes," *The New York Times*, August 7, 2012, http://www.nytimes.com/2012/08/08/business/global/frances-les-riches-vow-to-leave-if-75-tax-rate-is-passed.html?pagewanted=all.

148. Ibid.

149. Ibid.

150. Michael S. Schmidt and Edward Wyatt, "Corporate Fraud Cases Often Spare Individuals," *New York Times*, August 7,

2012, http://www.nytimes.com/2012/08/08/business/more-fraud-settlements-for-companies-but-rarely-individuals. html.

151. Clifford Krauss, "U.S. Reliance on Oil From Saudi Arabia is Growing Again," *New York Times* online, August 16, 2012, http://www.nytimes.com/2012/08/17/business/energy-environment/us-reliance-on-saudi-oil-is-growing-again. html?pagewanted=all.

152. Bojan Pancevski, "Saudis fund Balkan Muslims Spreading Hate of the West," *Sunday Times* (Europe), March 28, 2010, http://www.thesundaytimes.co.uk/sto/news/world_news/ Europe/article251901.ece.

153. Raymond Learsy, "'If You See Something Say Something' – The Failed Times Square Bombing and the Price of Oil," *Huffington Post* (blog), May 13, 2010, http://www.huffingtonpost.com/ raymond-j-learsy/if-you-see-something-say_b_574586.html.

154. John M. Broder, "An Inconvenient Statement, Retracted," *New York Times*, (blog), March 13, 2012, http://green.blogs.nytimes. com/2012/03/13/an-inconvenient-statement-retracted/.

155. Raymond Learsy, "Energy Secretary Chu and the Price You Are Paying for Gasoline," *Huffington Post* (blog), April 16, 2012, http://www.huffingtonpost.com/raymond-j-learsy/ energy-secretary-chu-and_b_1427999.html.

156. Peter Orszag, "Natural-Gas Cars Can Drive Us Toward a Better Economy," *Bloomberg*, June 26, 2012, http://www.bloomberg. com/news/2012-06-26/natural-gas-cars-can-drive-us-toward-a-better-economy.html.

157. Raymond Learsy, "Aspen Ideas, Natural Gas, Armenia Unheralded," *Huffington Post* (blog), July 9, 2012, http://www. huffingtonpost.com/raymond-j-learsy/aspen-ideas-natural-gas-a_b_1658566.html.

158. David Cho, "A Few Speculators Dominate Vast Market for Oil Trading," *The Washington Post*, August 21, 2008, http://www. washingtonpost.com/wp-dyn/content/article/2008/08/20/AR2008082003898.html.

159. Raymond Learsy, "Time to Dismiss the CFTC Chairman and His Commissioners," *Huffington Post* (blog), December 27, 2010, http://www.huffingtonpost.com/raymond-j-learsy/oil-over-90barrel--time-t_b_801451.html.

160. Senator Maria Cantwell, "Under Questioning by Cantwell, Exxon CEO Estimate Oil Should Cost $60–$70 Per Barrel," YouTube, accessed April 29, 2013, http://www.youtube.com/watch?v=LY420_U4U0I.

161. Raymond Learsy, "Are Our Leaders Hearing ExxonMobil CEO Tillerson?," *Huffington Post* (blog), May 17, 2011, http://www.huffingtonpost.com/raymond-j-learsy/attorney-general-holdercf_b_862873.html.

162. Camilla Hall and Henny Sender, "Qatar Holding Comes of Age as It Resists 'Glenstrata'," *Financial Times*, August 24, 2012, http://www.ft.com/intl/cms/s/0/74f2a9ba-ee03-11e1-a9d7-00144feab49a.html#axzz2OqUUHVhu.

163. Beth Greenfield, "The World's Richest Countries," *Forbes*, February 22, 2012, http://www.forbes.com/sites/bethgreenfield/2012/02/22/the-worlds-richest-countries/.

164. "Supranational union," *Wikipedia*, http://en.wikipedia.org/wiki/Supranational.

165. Ben Lando, "OPEC: NOPEC Bill Will Hurt US," United Press International (UPI), June 28, 2007, http://www.upi.com/Science_News/Resource-Wars/2007/06/28/OPEC-bill-will-hurt-US/UPI-29251183080388/.

166. Oil Price Reduction Act of 2000, S. 2182, 106th Congress (2000), http://www.govtrack.us/congress/bills/106/s2182#.

167. No Oil Producing and Exporting Cartels Act of 2007, S.879, 110th Congress (2007) http://www.govtrack.us/congress/bills/110/s879.

168. Herb Kohl, "Kohl's 'NOPEC' Bill to Protect U.S. Consumers From Oil Price Fixing Passes Senate Judiciary Committee," Votesmart.org, Apr. 7, 2011, http://votesmart.org/public-statement/600135/kohls-nopec-bill-to-protect-us-consumers-from-oil-price-fixing-passes-senate-judiciary-committee#. UVSq4Bn1e2A.

169. Juliet Chung and Jean Eaglesham, "Trades After 2008 Meeting Probed," *The Wall Street Journal*, September 13, 2012, http://online.wsj.com/article/SB10000872396390444433504577650082716565686.html?mod=googlenews_wsj.

170. Ibid.

171. Raymond Learsy, "Bailout Ballet: *New York Times* Reports on Hank Paulson/Pimco's Bill Gross Pas de Deux," *Huffington Post* (blog), September 26, 2008, http://www.huffingtonpost.com/raymond-j-learsy/bailout-balletnytimes-rep_b_129479.html.

172. Edward Wyatt, "For Hire: Bailout Advisor," *New York Times*, September 25, 2008, http://query.nytimes.com/gst/fullpage.h tml?res=9804E7DC113DF936A1575AC0A96E9C8B63&page wanted=all.

173. "Bailout for Billionaires," *The Wall Street Journal*, September 11, 2008, http://online.wsj.com/article/SB122108823814621239. html.

174. Raymond Learsy, "The Bailout: The Bond Billionaires Piggybacking The American Taxpayer For Another Gilded Ride," *Huffington Post* (blog), September 21, 2008, http://www. huffingtonpost.com/raymond-j-learsy/the-bailout-the-bond-bill_b_128036.html.

175. Nomi Prins, "Paulson's Revealing Phone Records," The Daily Beast, October 12, 2009, http://www.thedailybeast.com/ articles/2009/10/12/paulsons-revealing-phone-records.html.

176. Raymond Learsy, "The Key Question No One Asked About Goldman's Role In The AIG Bailout," *Huffington Post* (blog), November 20, 2009, http://www.huffingtonpost.com/raymond-j-learsy/key-question-unasked-unan_b_365119.html.

177. David D. Kirkpatrick and Steven Erlanger, "Egypt's New Leader Spells Out Terms for US-Arab Ties," *New York Times*, September 22, 2012, http://www.nytimes.com/2012/09/23/ world/middleeast/egyptian-leader-mohamed-morsi-spells-out-terms-for-us-arab-ties.html?pagewanted=all.

178. Leon Uris, *The Haj*, (New York: Bantam Books, 1985), 14.

179. Javier Blas, "Vitol Admits Iran Fuel Oil Cargo Deal," *Financial Times*, September 26, 2012, http://www.ft.com/ cms/s/0/220e4f34-07ed-11e2-a2d8-00144feabdc0.html.

180. Charles M. Blow, "Don't' Mess With Big Bird," *New York Times*, October 5, 2012, http://www.nytimes.com/2012/10/06/opinion/blow-dont-mess-with-big-bird.html.

181. Mitt Romney, "Romney: How I'll Tackle Spending, Debt," *USA Today*, November 3, 2011, http://usatoday30.usatoday.com/news/opinion/forum/story/2011-11-03/mitt-romney-budget-plan/51063454/1.

182. Michael Barbaro, "After a Romney Deal, Profits and Then Layoffs," *New York Times*, November 12, 2011, http://www.nytimes.com/2011/11/13/us/politics/after-mitt-romney-deal-company-showed-profits-and-then-layoffs.html?pagewanted=all.

183. Reuters, "IMF Chief Praises Gulf Effort on Oil Price Management," *Chicago Tribune*, October 6, 2012, http://articles.chicagotribune.com/2012-10-06/business/sns-rt-us-saudi-imf-crudebre89507a-20121006_1_imf-chief-christine-lagarde-oil-prices-bpd.

184. Chris Giles, "IMF Cuts Global Growth Forecast," *Financial Times*, January 23, 2013, http://www.ft.com/intl/cms/s/0/5dfc3ea8-6552-11e2-8b03-00144feab49a.html#axzz2OqUUHVhu.

185. Jad Mouawad, "Big Oil Projects Put in Jeopardy by Fall in Prices," *New York Times*, December 15, 2008, http://www.nytimes.com/2008/12/16/business/16oil.html?pagewanted=all.

186. Clifford Krauss and Eric Lipton, "After the Boom in Natural Gas," *New York Times* online, October 20, 2012, http://www.nytimes.com/2012/10/21/business/energy-environment/in-a-natural-gas-glut-big-winners-and-losers.html?pagewanted=all&_r=0.

187. Ian Urbina, "Insiders Sound an Alarm Amid a Natural Gas Rush," *New York Times*, June 25, 2011, http://www.nytimes.com/2011/06/26/us/26gas.html?pagewanted=all.

188. Ian Urbina, "Behind Veneer, Doubt on Future of Natural Gas," *New York Times*, June 26, 2011, http://www.nytimes.com/2011/06/27/us/27gas.html?pagewanted=all.

189. Raymond Learsy, "*The New York Times* Flays Natural Gas to the Cheers of the Oil Industry, OPEC, and Coal Producers," *Huffington Post* (blog), June 28, 2011, http://www.huffingtonpost.com/raymond-j-learsy/the-nytimes-flays-natural_b_886234.html.

190. Steven M. Davidoff, "Reading the Fine Print in Abacus and Other Soured Deals," *New York Times*, November 2, 2012, http://dealbook.nytimes.com/2012/11/02/reading-the-fine-print-in-abacus-and-other-soured-deals/.

191. Ibid.

192. Raymond Learsy, "*The New York Times*' Timely Whitewash of Goldman Sachs," *Huffington Post* (blog), June 18, 2010, http://www.huffingtonpost.com/raymond-j-learsy/the-new-york-times-timely_b_616953.html.

193. Raymond Learsy, "*The New York Times* Sheds a Tear for Wall Street Paydays," *Huffington Post* (blog), August 20, 2012, http://www.huffingtonpost.com/raymond-j-learsy/the-new-york-times-sheds_b_1411251.html.

194. Editorial, "The Junk Is Back in Junk Bonds," *New York Times*, November 1, 2012, http://www.nytimes.com/2012/11/02/opinion/the-junk-is-back-in-junk-bonds.html.

195. Edmund L. Andrews, "Reluctant Iran Falls in Line With OPEC Production Rise," *New York Times*, March 30, 2000, http://www.nytimes.com/2000/03/30/world/reluctant-iran-falls-in-line-with-opec-production-rise.html?src=pm.

196. Samuel R. Avro, "Energy Secretary Admits to Naïveté Over OPOEC Remarks," Energy Trends Insider, February 19, 2009, http://www.energytrendsinsider.com/2009/02/19/energy-secretary-admits-naivete-over-opec-remarks/.

197. John M. Broder, "An Inconvenient Statement, Retracted," *New York Times*, Green (blog), March 13, 2012, http://green.blogs.nytimes.com/2012/03/13/an-inconvenient-statement-retracted/.

198. Raymond Learsy, "President Obama Speaks and the Oil Speculators React," *Huffington Post* (blog), April 24, 2012, http://www.huffingtonpost.com/raymond-j-learsy/president-obama-speaks-an_b_1448280.html.

199. Guy Chazan and Ed Crooks, "US to Be World's Top Energy Producer," *Financial Times*, November 12, 2012, http://www.ft.com/intl/cms/s/0/8c2bcdf2-2c9f-11e2-9211-00144feabdc0.html#axzz2PFHCHv3V.

200. Fares Akram and Isabel Kershner, "Hamas Finds Itself Aligned with Israel Over Extremist Groups," *New York Times*, October 19, 2012, http://www.nytimes.com/2012/10/20/world/middleeast/hamas-works-to-suppress-militant-groups-in-gaza.html?_r=0.

201. Ibid.

202. Raymond Learsy, "Mr. Buffett's *New York Times'* Op-Ed. Thank You We Feel Better Now," *Huffington Post* (blog), November

17, 2010, http://www.huffingtonpost.com/raymond-j-learsy/
mr-buffets-new-york-times_b_784953.html.

203. Chris Isidore, "Buffett wants Jamie Dimon as Treasury
Secretary," CNNMoney, November 27, 2012, http://money.
cnn.com/2012/11/27/news/economy/buffett-dimon-treasury-
secretary/index.html.

204. Raymond Learsy, "Jamie Dimon's Malign Influence on the
Culture of American Banking," *Huffington Post* (blog), April
24, 2012, http://www.huffingtonpost.com/raymond-j-learsy/
jamie-dimons-malign-influ_b_1671325.html.

205. "Alleged Violations of The Servicemembers Civil Relief Act,"
Hearing before the Committee On Veterans' Affairs, U.S.
House of Representatives, 112 Congress, Feb 9, 2011 Serial No.
112-1, http://www.gpo.gov/fdsys/pkg/CHRG-112hhrg65867/
html/CHRG-112hhrg65867.htm.

206. Raymond Learsy, "It's All About the Money: Jamie Dimon's
Big Pay Hike and the Home Foreclosures of Our Servicemen,"
Huffington Post (blog), February 19, 2011, http://www.
huffingtonpost.com/raymond-j-learsy/its-all-about-the-
money-j_b_825485.html.

207. Raymond Learsy, "With Geithner's Replacement the Treasury
May Get a Woman's Touch," *Huffington Post* (blog), November
25, 2012, http://www.huffingtonpost.com/2012/11/25/
geithner-replacement-treasury_n_2170951.html.

208. Raymond Learsy, "America Needs A President Who Will
Confront the Financial Industry's Hegemony Over Our Lives,"
Huffington Post (blog), July 14, 2011, http://www.huffingtonpost.
com/raymond-j-learsy/america-needs-a-president_b_898047.
html.

209. Joe Nocera, "Sheila Bair's Bank Shot," *New York Times*, July 9, 2011, http://www.nytimes.com/2011/07/10/magazine/sheila-bairs-exit-interview.html?pagewanted=all&_r=0.

210. Soledad O'Brien, "Sheila Bair Endorses Elizabeth Warren," CNN Starting Point with Soledad O'Brien online transcripts, Aired Nov. 2, 2012 07:00 ET, accessed May 16, 2013, http://transcripts.cnn.com/TRANSCRIPTS/1211/02/sp.01.html.

211. Ibid.

212. Post Staff, "O Warns Syria," *New York Post*, December 4, 2012, http://www.nypost.com/p/news/international/warns_syria_CggO9X8cyPlAzPrkj7jlnK.

213. Javier Blas and Gregory Meyer, "Texas Crude Glut Sparks Oil Price Swings," *Financial Times*, December 3, 2012, http://www.ft.com/intl/cms/s/0/5958d14a-3af0-11e2-bb32-00144feabdc0.html.

214. Javier Blas, "Canada's Oil Now the Cheapest in the World," *Financial Times*, December 14, 2012, http://www.ft.com/intl/cms/s/0/551f58d0-4624-11e2-b780-00144feabdc0.html#axzz2PFHCHv3V.

215. Raymond Learsy, "Obama Administration Announces Formation of Oil/Gas Pricing Fraud Panel. Really?," *Huffington Post* (blog), April, 27, 2011, http://www.huffingtonpost.com/raymond-j-learsy/obama-administration-anno_b_854190.html.

216. Yoko Ono, letter to the editor, *New York Times*, December 25, 2012, http://www.nytimes.com/2012/12/26/opinion/concerns-about-the-safety-of-fracking.html.

217. "Yoko Ono, Sean Lennon put Anti-Fracking Message on New York Billboard," *Rolling Stone*, November 8, 2012, http://www.rollingstone.com/politics/news/yoko-ono-sean-lennon-put-anti-fracking-message-on-new-york-billboard-20121108.

218. Allison Sider, Russell Gold and Ben Lefebvre, "Drillers Begin Reusing 'Frack Water'," *The Wall Street Journal*, November 20, 2012, http://online.wsj.com/article/SB10001424052970203937 004578077183112409260.html.

219. Raymond Learsy, "Aspen Ideas, Natural Gas Armenia Unheralded," *Huffington Post* (blog), July 9, 2012, http://www.huffingtonpost.com/raymond-j-learsy/aspen-ideas-natural-gas-a_b_1658566.html.

220. Noel Sheppard, "Matt Damon's Anti-Fracking Film Backed by OPEC Nation," *NewsBusters* (blog), September 28, 2012, http://newsbusters.org/blogs/noel-sheppard/2012/09/28/matt-damons-anti-fracking-film-backed-opec-nation.

221. Javier Blas, "OPEC Cartel to Reap Record $1tn," *Financial Times*, December 30, 2012, http://www.ft.com/intl/cms/s/0/eedc5b56-50da-11e2-9623-00144feab49a.html#axzz2PFHCHv3V.

222. William Maclean and Barbara Lewis, "OPEC Makes Deepest Oil Cut Ever to Rescue Prices," *Reuters*, December 17, 2008, http://uk.reuters.com/article/2008/12/17/uk-opec-idUKFCA00012420081217.

223. Raymond Learsy, "'Noble' OPEC Criticizes the International Energy Agency," *Huffington Post* (blog), January 19, 2011, http://www.huffingtonpost.com/raymond-j-learsy/noble-opec-criticzes-the_b_810810.html.

224. Katrina Manson, "Extremism on the Rise in Zanzibar," *Financial Times*, December 28, 2012, http://www.ft.com/intl/cms/s/0/c85b0054-42c0-11e2-a4e4-00144feabdc0.html#axzz2H6an7yDj.

225. Adam Nossiter, "Jihadists' Fierce Justice Drives Thousands to Flee Mali," *New York Times*, July 17, 2012, http://www.nytimes.com/2012/07/18/world/africa/jidhadists-fierce-justice-drives-thousands-to-flee-mali.html?pagewanted=all&_r=1&.

226. Bojan Pancevski, "Saudis Fund Balkan Muslims Spreading Hate of the West," *The Sunday Times* (U.K.), March 28, 2010, http://www.thesundaytimes.co.uk/sto/news/world_news/Europe/article251901.ece.

227. Nelson D. Schwartz, "BP Loses Trading-Floor Swagger in Energy Markets," *New York Times*, June 27, 2010, http://www.nytimes.com/2010/06/28/business/global/28bptrade.html?dbk.

228. Raymond Learsy, "Yoko Ono, Matt Damon and OPEC Versus American Energy Independence," *Huffington Post* (blog), December 27, 2012, http://www.huffingtonpost.com/raymond-j-learsy/yoko-ono-matt-damon-and-o_b_2370464.html.

229. Raymond Learsy, "NOPEC ('No Oil Producing and Exporting Cartels'): A Presidential Issue and a Test of Political Integrity," *Huffington Post* (blog), September 10, 2012, http://www.huffingtonpost.com/raymond-j-learsy/nopec-no-oil-producing-an_b_1869803.html.

230. Brian Baskin and Ben Lefebvre, "Chevron's Email 'Oops' Reveals Energy Giant's Sway Over Markets," *The Wall Street Journal*, July 16, 2011, http://online.wsj.com/article/SB10001424052702304521304576448202801087220.html.

231. Edmund L. Andrews, "Reluctant Iran Falls in Line With OPEC Production Rise," *New York Times*, March 30, 2000, http://www.nytimes.com/2000/03/30/world/reluctant-iran-falls-in-line-with-opec-production-rise.html?src=pm.

232. Samuel R. Avro, "Energy Secretary Admits to Naiveté Over OPEC Remarks," Energy Trends Insider, February 19, 2009, http://www.energytrendsinsider.com/2009/02/19/energy-secretary-admits-naivete-over-opec-remarks/.

233. Raymond Learsy, "Are Our Leaders Hearing ExxonMobil CEO Tillerson?," *Huffington Post* (blog), May 17, 2011, http://www.huffingtonpost.com/raymond-j-learsy/attorney-general-holdercf_b_862873.html.

234. Raymond Learsy, "Aspen Ideas, Natural Gas, Armenia Unheralded," *Huffington Post* (blog), July 9, 2012, http://www.huffingtonpost.com/raymond-j-learsy/aspen-ideas-natural-gas-a_b_1658566.html.

235. Scott Rose and Olga Tanas, "Putin Turns Black Gold to Bullion as Russia Outbuys World," *Bloomberg*, February 11, 2013, http://www.bloomberg.com/news/2013-02-10/putin-turns-black-gold-into-bullion-as-russia-out-buys-world.html.

236. United States Commodity Futures Trading Commission, "CFTC Sanctions ConAgra Trade Group, Inc. $12 Million for Causing a Non-Bona Fide Price to Be Reported in the NYMEX Crude Oil Futures Contract," August 16, 2010, http://www.cftc.gov/PressRoom/PressReleases/pr5873-10.

237. Raymond Learsy, "Oil Embargoes, Sherlock Holmes, and the Russian Butler," *Huffington Post* (blog), February 20, 2012, http://www.huffingtonpost.com/raymond-j-learsy/oil-embargoessherlock-hol_b_1288687.html.

238. Raymond Learsy, "The Oil Market Plays Casino While the Obama Administration Acts as Croupier," *Huffington Post* (blog), September 19, 2011, http://www.huffingtonpost.com/raymond-j-learsy/the-oil-market-plays-casi_b_969251.html.

239. Spectrum Store, Inc, et.al. v. CITGO Petroleum Corporation, et. al., United States Court of Appeals for the Fifth Circuit, No. 09-20084, filed February 8, 2001, http://www.ca5.uscourts.gov/opinions%5Cpub%5C09/09-20084-CV0.wpd.pdf.

240. Raymond Learsy, "NOPEC ('No Oil Producing and Exporting Cartels'): A Presidential Issue and a Test of Political Integrity," *Huffington Post* (blog), September 10, 2012, http://www.huffingtonpost.com/raymond-j-learsy/nopec-no-oil-producing-an_b_1869803.html.

241. "President Obama on Automatic Spending Cuts," C-Span (video), March 1, 2013, accessed May 13, 2013, http://www.c-spanvideo.org/videoLibrary/transcript/transcript.php?programid=303097.

242. Raymond Learsy, "Obama's Middle Class Dream Touted in Inaugural Speech Still Far from Reality," *Huffington Post* (blog), January 21, 2013, http://www.huffingtonpost.com/2013/01/21/obama-middle-class_n_2521082.html.

243. Raymond Learsy, "Obama Calls Sequester Cuts 'Dumb' and 'Arbitrary,' Blames GOP for Inflexibility," *Huffington Post* (blog), March 1, 2013, http://www.huffingtonpost.com/2013/03/01/obama-sequester-cuts_n_2790040.html.

244. Jessica Silver-Greenberg and Ben Protess, "JPMorgan Faulted on Controls and Disclosure in Trading Loss," *New York Times*, March 14, 2013, http://dealbook.nytimes.com/2013/03/14/

jpmorgan-faulted-on-controls-and-disclosure-in-trading-loss/.

245. Raymond Learsy, "Our Next Secretary of the Treasury: A Woman or Jamie Dimon," *Huffington Post* (blog), November 28, 2012, http://www.huffingtonpost.com/raymond-j-learsy/our-next-secretary-of-the_b_2202868.html.

246. Raymond Learsy, "Banks in Collusion with the Fed Shamelessly Spike Up Price of Oil/Gasoline," *Huffington Post* (blog), July 18, 2012, http://www.huffingtonpost.com/raymond-j-learsy/the-banks-in-collusion-wi_b_1681685.html.

247. Raymond Learsy, "Jamie Dimon's Malign Influence on the Culture of American Banking," *Huffington Post* (blog), July 13, 2012, http://www.huffingtonpost.com/raymond-j-learsy/jamie-dimons-malign-influ_b_1671325.html.

248. Raymond Learsy, "The *Wall Street Journal's* Convoluted Whitewash of Jamie Dimon," *Huffington Post* (blog), May 14, 2012, http://www.huffingtonpost.com/raymond-j-learsy/the-wall-street-journals_b_1516393.html.

249. Raymond Learsy, "The Volcker Rule and Wall Street's Pliant Media Plant," *Huffington Post* (blog), February 15, 2012, http://www.huffingtonpost.com/raymond-j-learsy/the-volcker-rule-and-wall_b_1278419.html.

250. Raymond Learsy, "Alan Greenspan Tells it Like it Isn't," *Huffington Post* (blog), June 25, 2012, http://www.huffingtonpost.com/raymond-j-learsy/alan-greenspan-tells-it-l_b_1623275.html.

251. Raymond Learsy, "Bravo JPMorgan! Just What We Need, Another Wall Street Casino," *Huffington Post* (blog), October

12, 2010, http://www.huffingtonpost.com/raymond-j-learsy/bravo-jp-morgan-just-what_b_759262.html.

252. Raymond Learsy, "JPMorgan Shows Us the Volcker Rule is all Hat and No Cattle While the Administration and Congress Fiddle Away," *Huffington Post* (blog), February 16, 2010, http://www.huffingtonpost.com/raymond-j-learsy/jpmorgan-shows-us-the-vol_b_463804.html.

253. Raymond Learsy, "Did the Huffington Post Bring JPMorgan Chase to Heel?," *Huffington Post* (blog), February 2, 2010, http://www.huffingtonpost.com/raymond-j-learsy/did-the-huffington-post-b_b_445629.html.

254. Raymond Learsy, "JPMorgan Chase Throws Down the Gauntlet at President Obama," *Huffington Post* (blog), January 26, 2010, http://www.huffingtonpost.com/raymond-j-learsy/jpmorgan-chase-throws-dow_b_436572.html.

255. Raymond Learsy, "Our Banks Becoming Casinos and Washington Yawns," *Huffington Post* (blog), January 20, 2010, http://www.huffingtonpost.com/raymond-j-learsy/our-banks-becoming-casino_b_429410.html.

256. Raymond Learsy, "Is JPMorgan a Bank or a Government-Funded Casino?," *Huffington Post* (blog), June 9, 2009, http://www.huffingtonpost.com/raymond-j-learsy/is-jp-morgan-a-bank-or-a_b_212971.html.

257. Raymond Learsy, "Wall Street Banks Blindsided Gambling with Monies Entrusted to Them," *Huffington Post* (blog), June 16, 2009, http://www.huffingtonpost.com/raymond-j-learsy/wall-street-banks-blindsi_b_216042.html.

258. Jessica Silver-Greenberg, "JPMorgan Board Confirms Dual Role for Dimon," *New York Times*, March 22, 2013, http://dealbook.nytimes.com/2013/03/22/jpmorgan-board-says-dimon-should-remain-as-c-e-o-and-chairman/.

259. Raymond Learsy, "Jamie Dimon's Malign Influence on the Culture of American Banking," *Huffington Post* (blog), July 13, 2012, http://www.huffingtonpost.com/raymond-j-learsy/jamie-dimons-malign-influ_b_1671325.html.

260. Raymond Learsy, "Exxon's Lee Raymond, 'Steward of the Free Market System," *Huffington Post* (blog), April 15, 2006, http://www.huffingtonpost.com/raymond-j-learsy/exxons-lee-raymond-stewar_b_19197.html.

261. David D. Kirkpatrick, "Short of Money, Egypt Sees Crisis on Fuel and Food," *New York Times*, March 30, 2013, http://www.nytimes.com/2013/03/31/world/middleeast/egypt-short-of-money-sees-crisis-on-food-and-gas.html?pagewanted=all&_r=0.

262. Heba Saleh and Emiko Terazono, "Egypt Seeks Better Deal for Wheat Imports," *Financial Times*, March 26, 2013, http://www.ft.com/intl/cms/s/0/781f945e-9560-11e2-a4fa-00144feabdc0.html.

263. Jack Farchy, "US Drought a Bounty for Dreyfus," *Financial Times*, March 27, 2013, http://www.ft.com/intl/cms/s/0/5e8fdad6-96fe-11e2-8950-00144feabdc0.html.

264. Emiko Terazono, "Swiss Review Supports Commodities Trading," *Financial Times*, March 27, 2013, http://www.ft.com/intl/cms/s/0/f110aa02-96ef-11e2-a77c-00144feabdc0.html.

265. Javier Blas, "Vitol Expands into Grains Trading," *Financial Times,* April 2, 2013, http://www.ft.com/intl/cms/s/0/af3a4468-9bad-11e2-a820-00144feabdc0.html#axzz2Rt23Hkbm.

266. Dan Strumpf and Jenny Gross, "Traders Slip on Brent Oil Bet," *Wall Street Journal*, April 18, 2013, http://online.wsj.com/article/SB10001424127887324763404578430790299285154.html.

267. Raymond Learsy, "Commodity Exchanges Prime the Pump for Higher Oil/Gasoline Prices," *Huffington Post* (blog), May 31, 2012, http://www.huffingtonpost.com/raymond-j-learsy/commodity-exchanges-prime_b_1558801.html.

268. Raymond Learsy, "Oil Price Skyrockets 9.36 Percent in Friday's Trading, Supply and Demand Eh??," *Huffington Post* (blog), July 02, 2012, http://www.huffingtonpost.com/raymond-j-learsy/oil-price-skyrockets-936_b_1643325.html.

269. Raymond Learsy, "Are Our Leaders Hearing ExxonMobil CEO Tillerson?," *Huffington Post* (blog), May 17, 2011, http://www.huffingtonpost.com/raymond-j-learsy/attorney-general-holdercf_b_862873.html.

270. Raymond Learsy, "Oil Speculation at Chevron Laid Bare for All to See," *Huffington Post* (blog), July 20, 2011, http://www.huffingtonpost.com/raymond-j-learsy/oil-speculation-at-chevro_b_904289.html.

271. Raymond Learsy, "BP's Smoking Gun and the Manipulation of Oil Prices," *Huffington Post* (blog), June 30, 2010, http://www.huffingtonpost.com/raymond-j-learsy/bps-smoking-gun-and-the-m_b_630275.html.

272. Raymond Learsy, "The Trade That Brought Us $100/barrel Oil Teaches Us to Be Afraid, Be Very Afraid," *Huffington Post* (blog), January 7, 2008, http://www.huffingtonpost.com/raymond-j-learsy/the-trade-that-brought-us_1_b_80149.html.

Index

Page numbers containing "*n*" and "*nn*" refer to notes.

CPSIA information can be obtained at www.ICGtesting.com
Printed in the USA
LVOW06s0712310713

345429LV00002B/166/P